www.wadsworth.com

www.wadsworth.com is the World Wide Web site for Wadsworth and is your direct source to dozens of online resources.

At *www.wadsworth.com* you can find out about supplements, demonstration software, and student resources. You can also send email to many of our authors and preview new publications and exciting new technologies.

www.wadsworth.com
Changing the way the world learns®

Skin and Bones

Skin and Bones

The Management of People and Natural Resources in Shellcracker Haven, Florida

Jane W. Gibson
University of Kansas
Lawrence, Kansas

 Case Studies in Cultural Anthropology: George Spindler, Series Editor

THOMSON
WADSWORTH

Australia • Canada • Mexico • Singapore • Spain
United Kingdom • United States

Anthropology Editor: *Lin Marshall*
Assistant Editor: *Nicole Root*
Editorial Assistant: *Kelly McMahon*
Marketing Manager: *Diane Wenckebach*
Marketing Assistant: *Tara Pierson*
Advertising Project Manager: *Linda Yip*
Project Manager, Editorial Production:
  Jennifer Klos

Print/Media Buyer: *Rebecca Cross*
Permissions Editor: *Sarah Harkrader*
Production Service: *Buuji, Inc.*
Copy Editor: *Linda Ireland, Buuji, Inc.*
Cover Designer: *Rob Hugel*
Cover Image: *Jack Dequine*
Text and Cover Printer: *Webcom*
Compositor: *Buuji, Inc.*

The logo for the Cultural Anthropology series is based on an ancient symbol representing the family: man, woman, and children.

Printed in Canada
1 2 3 4 5 6 7 08 07 06 05 04 03

For more information about our products,
contact us at:
Thomson Learning Academic Resource Center
1-800-423-0563

For permission to use material from this text,
contact us by:
Phone: 1-800-730-2214   **Fax:** 1-800-730-2215
Web: http://www.thomsonrights.com

Library of Congress Control Number: 2003112649

ISBN 0-15-508476-3

Wadsworth/Thomson Learning
10 Davis Drive
Belmont, CA 94002-3098
USA

Asia
Thomson Learning
5 Shenton Way #01-01
UIC Building
Singapore 068808

Australia/New Zealand
Thomson Learning
102 Dodds Street
Southbank, Victoria 3006
Australia

Canada
Nelson
1120 Birchmount Road
Toronto, Ontario M1K 5G4
Canada

Europe/Middle East/Africa
Thomson Learning
High Holborn House
50/51 Bedford Row
London WC1R 4LR
United Kingdom

Latin America
Thomson Learning
Seneca, 53
Colonia Polanco
11560 Mexico D.F.
Mexico

Spain/Portugal
Paraninfo
Calle/Magallanes, 25
28015 Madrid, Spain

*To Jack Dequine and the families of Shellcracker Haven,
and to Caleb, Taylor, and Lily*

Contents

Foreword

ABOUT THE SERIES

These case studies in cultural anthropology are designed for students in beginning and intermediate courses in the social sciences, to bring them insights into the richness and complexity of human life as it is lived in different ways, in different places. The authors are men and women who have lived in the societies they write about and who are professionally trained as observers and interpreters of human behavior. Also, the authors are teachers; in their writing, the needs of the student reader remain foremost. It is our belief that when an understanding of ways of life very different from one's own is gained, abstractions and generalizations about the human condition become meaningful.

The scope and character of the series has changed constantly since we published the first case studies in 1960, in keeping with our intention to represent anthropology as it is. We are concerned with the ways in which human groups and communities are coping with the massive changes wrought in their physical and sociopolitical environments in recent decades. We are also concerned with the ways in which established cultures have solved life's problems. And we want to include representation of the various modes of communication and emphasis that are being formed and reformed as anthropology itself changes.

We think of this series as an instructional series, intended for use in the classroom. We, the editors, have always used case studies in our teaching, whether for beginning students or advanced graduate students. We start with case studies, whether from our own series or from elsewhere, and weave our way into theory, and then turn again to cases. For us, they are the grounding of our discipline.

ABOUT THE AUTHOR

Jane Gibson studied at Baylor University, earning an MS in environmental studies, and the University of Florida where she completed her doctorate in anthropology. Her work has focused on the ways humans think about and relate to the natural world, particularly as these relationships are mediated by institutional changes associated with conservation and development. She currently teaches at the University of Kansas, where her present research explores the impacts of ecotourism on host community families and ecosystems in Costa Rica.

ABOUT THIS CASE STUDY

Shellcracker Haven is like no other place in America and like every place in America. It is like no other place in that it has its own unique history, stretching from 1842 to the present. It is like every place in that it sits at the intersection of natural resource management embattled by global, national, and regional forces stemming from a world in the thrall of development.

The history of Shellcracker Haven is a part of the history of a region character-ized by pine and oak woods, wetlands and lakes, and wildlife characteristic of wood-lands and freshwaters. Among many species, it has catfish, panfish, deer, wild hogs and turkeys, and alligators. The residents of Shellcracker Haven have harvested all of them, as well as crops from citrus groves and farmlands surrounding the commu-nity, moss hanging from cypress trees, and wood products from the forests. In brief, the residents of Shellcracker Haven have lived from the land and waters of Florida within which their community is physically, politically, and culturally embedded. For this reason, the people living there are particularly subject to pressures emanating from occupation and development of wild and "unincorporated" rural areas of the state.

This case study expresses the contradiction between conservation of the natural world and development of it. It is about power and money, bureaucratic and family loyalties, and love of place. Shellcracker Haven sits with those who struggle against population increase, housing developments, and other commercial interests that threaten the life-sustaining world. Yet Shellcracker Haven has had to adapt to new rules and laws governing the exploitation of natural resources, rules that threaten the bond families feel for this place, a bond that grows from experience as well as the living memories of ancestors now buried in the local cemetery, and a bond that has protected their "home" from corporate opportunists. The story is complicated by val-ues long operating in American culture and elsewhere in the developing world—placing human interests at the apex, with the needs of other species decidedly subordinate, disregarding the network of life for the singular purpose of a given proj-ect, such as housing or commercial development, and placing monetary profit as the major or only purpose of any and every enterprise.

Today Shellcracker Haven hangs onto its way of life and its love of place. Families still fish and hunt and harvest alligators, despite the hardships of so earning a living, but for how long? It is good to get to know this way of life before it disap-pears. It is good to consider that we all stand at the same crossroad where we can choose to continue fouling our planetary nest, or we can choose to love the world and live sustainably within it. This case study gives us a chance to know another way to "be" in the world, and to think about the choices we can make for ourselves and our descendants.

George Spindler
Series Editor
Stanford University
geospinner@aol.com

Preface

How we think about the natural world conditions how we live in it. Many years ago, I read *The Forest People,* Colin Turnbull's book about the Mbuti pygmies of the Ituri Forest. The Mbuti thought of the forest as a benevolent parent-provider, and they related to each other as siblings who must show their "parent" respect and affection. Mbuti and forest continued in what appeared to be a sustainable relationship, at least until outsiders found ways to encourage Mbuti to intensify their hunting efforts.

By contrast, a mainstream view of the relationship between people and the natural world held by North Americans sets nature and culture apart and prioritizes the needs of people over all other species, and the needs of some people over others. These views are very old but are culturally specific, as they have been shaped by neoclassical economic theory and capitalism, now morphed into a national, secular religion. We Americans live in a world that assigns value to the biosphere in the marketplace. Here, to the extent that something can be extracted, processed, and sold, it has value. Trees are a source of wood for furniture, paper, and the construction industry. Elephants produce ivory, leather, and umbrella stands. A piece of ground produces corn or pasture for cattle, which are valued for milk, meat, and hides. In the end, under this ideological and economic system, the ecosystem falls apart, first metaphorically because it is seen as being made up of discrete parts and potential commodities. It is a set of natural *resources.* And without the brakes put on by those who share access to these resources or by others concerned with conservation, the ecosystem falls apart, literally, because the extraction of component parts fails to take into consideration that system parts are interdependent. Whether or not we are willing to recognize the wisdom of the Mbuti, we too are embedded in the natural world, not separate from it, and when the natural world is in trouble, so are we.

This book about Shellcracker Haven, Florida, is a case study of a small community and the rise of state-level, science-based natural resource management. The agency's decisions profoundly affect the livelihoods of commercial fishing and hunting families in the community and in the state as it pursues its conservation mission. Yet, in spite of its constitutional authority and mission to conserve Florida's fish and wildlife, the Florida Fish and Wildlife Conservation Commission is powerless to stop the overwhelming processes that degrade and destroy species habitats. In Florida, the main culprits are development and urban expansion into rural areas, made highly profitable under the state's rapid population growth. But whether we are talking about poor people who are desperate for land, as in the Amazon, or the 700 mostly middle-class people who migrate to "the sunshine state" each day, the wild places on our planet, where the multitude of species make their homes, are being converted into a habitat for one.

What Shellcracker Haven offers us in the face of looming ecological disaster is another possibility for living in the world without destroying it. Here, families continue to live from small-scale commercial hunting and fishing. They live off the land,

and they live in it. While they are not "children of the forest" by any means, they are rooted in their natural world by history, shared memories, and traditions. And they have proven their affection for their "home" and way of life by standing against a powerful company when it would do harm to the lake and their social world.

We learn from Shellcracker Haven that culture and biological diversity are linked because people are embedded in the natural world, and because we are the dominant mammal, the predator of predators, and the only species that votes. And we learn that though the problems of ecological destruction are serious and the need for action urgent, communities like Shellcracker Haven persist through flexibility, resilience, and creativity. They adjust to changing circumstances while preserving the social ties that bind them to each other and to the basin in which they live. Here is a natural resource, a natural ally for those of us serious about conservation: the Florida Fish and Wildlife Conservation Commission, environmentalists, sports hunters and fishers, and environmental anthropologists. The people of Shellcracker Haven have experienced painful setbacks over the years, yet they bounce back like prizefighters who refuse to give up. The community is a worthy example for all of us.

ACKNOWLEDGMENTS

This book is the result of contributions made by many people. Jack Dequine, who is featured on the cover and to whom this work is dedicated, is owed more than words can express, not only for the support and assistance he gave to me, but for his courageous defense of the truth and the livelihoods of commercial fishing families. Jack, you were way ahead of your time. The families of Shellcracker Haven kindly endured my endless questions, presence, cameras, and tape recorders. My gratitude goes to all of them, but especially to those who appear by pseudonym in this book. Managers, biologists, and wildlife officers of the Florida Fish and Wildlife Conservation Commission made time for me and generously provided introductions and access to reports and data, and they made it possible for me to observe and videotape an alligator hunt. I must also thank Dave Roesner for his skills with a video camera, without which the resources I had available to me would not have been so rich. I give special thanks to Paul Doughty, mentor and friend, who encouraged me to publish *Skin and Bones,* and to my editor George Spindler, whose comments and suggestions improved the book immeasurably. I'd also like to thank Linda Ireland whose copyedits helped me say better what I wanted to say; Kelly McMahon for editorial assistance, but especially for support and encouragement; Jennifer Klos for project management; and Mary Deeg who deftly saw both me and the book through the production process. Finally, to my best friend and husband, Jim, and to my family, who forgive, love, support, and help me in all things, I remain happily indebted. In the end, credit for whatever redeems this effort goes to all those mentioned here. All its shortcomings are mine.

1/Meet Shellcracker Haven

INTRODUCTION

The years following World War II brought prosperity to America's growing industrial economy and higher incomes for many modernizing families. Not so in Shellcracker Haven, Florida, where a political struggle was waged and lost, leaving the families of the community to fall on hard times. Some name that period in their lives "the starvin' time."

In 1882, Shellcracker Haven was identified as a "pine woods" settlement (Myers 1882), and in 1888 it was referred to as a "landing and shipping point" (Ashby 1888). Today, the few outsiders who know of the tiny community at all know it as a poor fishing community where alligator hunters live, and even fewer know how it came to be the settlement that it is. Instead, they offer the conventional wisdom that blames the poor for their misfortune.

Community residents acknowledge local poverty, but they see their lives more broadly than the economic lens reveals. The town's senior residents share living memories of several dramatic transformations during Shellcracker Haven's 150-year history, offering a different explanation for low incomes. These views are set in the context of a world defined by kinship rather than competition.

The first settlers arrived under the 1842 Armed Occupation Act. They and early descendants were yeoman family farmers before the Great Depression, and their community was organized alongside a small neighborhood of company-owned shacks called the **still quarters** where black turpentiners lived. When the company moved the black community to another stand of pine trees near another town, the farm economy of Shellcracker Haven collapsed without the labor of the black women and children. Then commercial fishers lost the hotly contested battle over management of Florida's freshwater fisheries, so this source of income, too, dropped precipitously. The Florida Game and Fresh Water Fish Commission (GFC) rose from the ashes of this struggle. Today, it is named the Florida Fish and Wildlife Conservation Commission (FWC) and is still the agency that constitutes the most important overseer of Shellcracker Haven family livelihoods and Florida biodiversity.

1

Shellcracker Haven's history is important for its elders to tell, not only because it is their past and present, but also because it is the story played out in America's Appalachian and Ozark regions and in rural areas in many parts of the world. Globalization of market economies has extended those forces felt in Shellcracker Haven from the Australian outback to the Amazon. Now some Floridians, Aborigines, and Amazonian tribes share the same market niche as producers of raw **crocodilian** hides for the world fashion industry. All also feel the weight of state authorities in what were once traditional, subsistence activities.

The ability of many people in the world today to meet their basic needs and to feed their children is still tied to local access to and control over natural resources. In some cases, these have been lost to corporations bent on profit. In others, state institutions acting "for the public good" have separated families from their livelihoods. Always the taking involves the imposition of different views about the natural world and how people ought to live in it. This is a story about the clash of these different worldviews and agendas in a competitive economic and political landscape, where power is distributed unequally, disputes divide winners from losers, and losers are seen by those who do not know history to get their just desserts. And it is a story that holds out the possibility that we can learn from communities like Shellcracker Haven how to live on the planet without destroying it.

OUTSIDER

I decided to learn more about Shellcracker Haven through a study of food networks, particularly those built around **subsistence** fishing and hunting. One day, as I waited for my next interview in a health clinic north of the community, a nurse whispered to me, "There are alligator hunters down there." The implied stigma attached to this **livelihood strategy** peaked my interest, so I made it a point to visit the library to read about the area's history. When I asked the librarian for any information on the town, she warned me that I should be careful about where I went and to whom I spoke. Residents had a reputation for being a rough bunch, prone to occasional violence. Of course, I thought, I have to go there.

In the late summer of 1987, I began visiting Shellcracker Haven to learn about the community's involvement in Florida's Alligator Management Program. I attended alligator hunts and visited with the Knight family, best known and most highly recommended by members of the FWC for their experience as hunters. I made other acquaintances as well, videotaped and interviewed all who would permit it, and shared my interest in residence to improve my ability to learn about the community. I was especially interested in local history, in particular, families' continued reliance on hunting and fishing. After two years of these visits, I moved my family into a sweltering trailer on Shellcracker Lake to begin a year of intensive field research. I learned quickly that the community's tolerance for the presence of outsiders who come and go would not apply equally well to outsiders who come and stay. Living outside meant some minimum of access to people, places, and ideas for me and maximum control for them. Living "inside" meant crossing a line, coming too close, and staying too long.

I've thought about the community's thick carapace often in years since. What I now know is that they had much experience with powerful outsiders such as the sheriff's department, social services, and wildlife officers. From the local point of view,

Jane W. Gibson

I lived here for a year with my husband, Jim, and our daughters. We spent much of our time outside, where breezes blew across the lake and kept us cool.

none of these unwelcome intruders approached the community with the intention of making life better or easier. Out of this history arose the local belief that no one really cares about the people of Shellcracker Haven, that is, unless there is something to be gained at the locals' expense. Compared to these painful "visits" by powerful state institutions, I was easily managed with such tactics as simple lying, a source of great local amusement; frequent assertions that they "don't know nothing" or "can't tell you nothing"; occasional rudeness; veiled threats, echoing the librarian's, about places I shouldn't go and dangerous people I should avoid; and silence.

I had arrived in a state of naiveté about cultural difference and sameness. We looked alike, spoke the same language, and shared certain aspects of cultural heritage. But I did not share their social position in the larger society, nor important experiences, and I had no locally recognized ties to the community-kinship and permanent residence in particular. I grew up in a family that valued education and saw to mine. The parents and children of Shellcracker Haven rarely obtained their high school diplomas, and most saw education as irrelevant to their needs. And though we all spoke English, they spoke a distinctive dialect, one that set them apart from others and marked them as members, and me as an outsider. These and other differences served as a constant reminder of the histories, values, and, more importantly, the expectations we did not share. I would eventually leave for a very different life somewhere else.

I resolved to stop asking questions and to keep my distance as ways to show the people of Shellcracker Haven the respect they required. I also took on a part-time job as a stringer for the "Good News" section of the regional newspaper. I could carry pen and paper without raising the usual questions about what I "really" wanted to

know, and I took and shared photographs in my new role. The stories I wrote about
Aunt Zea's visit from Jacksonville, Stella's birthday party, and the church "sing"
were read by everyone. After a couple of months, the door opened at a church pic-
nic, and Mrs. Knight stepped out onto the church steps. She asked how my research
was going, and effectively invited me into their world. In return, I have done what I
could to protect the privacy of the community and its members. The names I have
used for the places and people are pseudonyms, and I have selected images that are
unlikely to be recognized outside Shellcracker Haven; time has passed and changed
the people themselves, and some are no longer living. Most importantly, because so
much of my research was preserved on video- and audiotape, community members
tell their own stories in this text wherever possible. Where my voice dominates, I
have tried to tell the truth as I understand it.

SCRATCHING THE SURFACE

Most of the houses of Shellcracker Haven sit tightly clustered behind a narrow tract
of trees just off the highway that divides the town into eastern and western halves.
The first settler families farmed the east, where some of their descendants live in
most of the widely dispersed houses. Small ponds formed from old "barrow pits," or
holes left where soil was removed, dot the area in which a multinational paper company owns large tracts of cultivated pines in and among locally owned farms. Trees
reached the end of their twenty-year growth cycle in 1990 when clear-cutting began,
a process that dramatically changed the face of the woodland community.

The county maintains graded roads that connect families to the Methodist church,
built by their ancestors from locally grown and milled trees. The church sits on land
donated in the late 19th century and is a source of pride in Shellcracker Haven.

South of the church sits a well-maintained, whites-only cemetery where the first
settlers, Civil War veterans, and those who came later are buried. It is separated from
the black cemetery by a fence and a gravel road. Families from the still quarters are
buried in the black cemetery; only the rise and fall of the land tells where they were
laid to rest.

The western half of the town is divided by the railroad track that parallels the
highway and Shellcracker Lake. This track separates the more expensive lake-front
property, mostly used for vacations by absentee owners, from resident descendants
of the town's first commercial fishing families, the post office, and the town's few
remaining businesses: a beauty salon, a boat repair shop, and a garage for car and
truck repair. Trains still run day and night through the middle of this mostly residen-
tial area, blasting a long warning chord each time they pass.

Two other areas complete the physical layout of the town, though there's no
agreement about where the unincorporated settlement begins and ends. Continuing
north along the lake edge, a public dock marks the edge of a county-owned park. The
dock affords convenient lake access to both sports and subsistence fishers from outside Shellcracker Haven. The paved road and parking area leading to it offer parking
for these occasional visitors and for visitors to the library's bookmobile. Other than
the occasional reader and children playing around the dock, the park area holds little
interest for residents of the town.

North of the park lies the newest extension of Shellcracker Haven. Red's Fish
Camp is owned by a professional baseball player and is run by his father. It stretches

Jane W. Gibson

This store sits across the street from the original building. Until it closed in 1991, it remained in the same family from the time before the Great Depression, and neighbors could buy there on credit, especially when times were hard.

along the lake edge marked by cabins, trailers, and the clubhouse. Red's abuts a housing development at Shellcracker Haven's most northern extreme, and both attract migrant "snowbirds." Some come for the winter to join resident retirees, many of whom started out as postharvest vacationers from the midwestern farm belt. These newer residents are not without their influence on natural resource management decisions.

EVERYBODY'S KIN

Kinship is the basic framework for social organization in all societies. It links people across generations so that knowledge is passed from parents to children, and it ties people of the same generation together in a web of mutual obligations and privileges. Daniel Bates wrote that kinship is the first system into which a person is introduced at birth, and it may be the only system of roles that remains unchanged throughout life (1996:208).

In Shellcracker Haven, visitors hear that "everybody's kin," and with only a few exceptions, the statement is true as Americans reckon kinship through biology and marriage. The community is woven together by other factors as well. Families are bound to each other by close physical proximity, shared memories, a community identity as hunters and fishers, and their history of "run-ins" with authorities of the state, which have contributed to the closed, defensive posture I encountered.

When needs arise, family members look to each other for assistance. Indeed, were it not for the social and economic safety net provided by this close-knit community to its members, it seems unlikely the town would have survived its difficult history. Families helped each other through the hardest times, and they continue to provide labor, child care, money, fuel, food, and housing to their members.

The extended family constitutes most of the social world, whether in the tiny Methodist church or someone's front yard. Men, women, and children share the excitement of a "gator" hunt or an unusually large catfish hauled in early that morning, and they share each other's troubled and happy memories. Kinfolk provide information about opportunities for hunting or making money, and they pass along to their children what is important in life and what being a member of the family entails: loyalty, mutual support, and protection from outsiders.

Mrs. Knight's daughter, Elaine, does not worry when her grandchildren walk alone through the neighborhood because everyone is well known and most are trusted relatives. Mrs. Knight left once many years ago, climbing onto the back of her husband's motorcycle to try a life in Houston, but she insisted they come home. As she tells the story, "We got there and I told him to turn right around and come back. I wouldn't be nowheres else but here." *Here* is where her father helped build the church and the house in which she and her siblings grew up, and it is where a baby brother died. It is where her husband and father built her present home and where she raised her two children. It is where her granddaughter now raises Mrs. Knight's first great-grandchildren, who occupy themselves with toys in a playpen set in the corner of the skinning shed while the rest of the family turn alligators into valuable hides and meat.

Though there is no official count and disagreements over boundaries remain, the population of the town, according to the local postmaster, has stabilized at around 450. Most of these people live in the farming and fishing sections defined primarily by one family (over half belong to the Knight clan) and a few elderly descendants of the town's first settlers.

Like many rural towns in America, Shellcracker Haven's population is aging, most noticeably on the farm side where most are retired seniors. They have either grown old here as their children moved away after marriage or to find work when farming declined, or they are people who left early and returned after retirement to live on their family's land. Mrs. Jameson, who was born in Shellcracker Haven early in the 20th century, stayed there after her farm collapsed, her husband was killed in a hunting accident, and her children moved away. She is so closely tied to her place in the world that she claims never to have ventured into the fishing community.

A few households contain younger couples and their small children, but most of these are related to members of the fishing community whose primary land base lies near the lake. The age structure of the farm side is top-heavy, reflecting the generalized decline in family farming in the United States and the particular situation of small farms in rural Florida and Shellcracker Haven.

The fishing families of Shellcracker Haven present a different picture. Four generations of Knights live near the lake, ranging from newborn babies to their elderly great-grandparents. Five brothers, their two sisters, all their spouses, and their spouses' siblings represent most of the oldest generation of Knights living today in the town. The five brothers' wives came from outside Shellcracker Haven, but the sisters married local men. The sister of a fisherman married a local farmer, thereby linking the farming and fishing communities and making economic opportunities available to the extended network of relatives.

Jane W. Gibson

Children become what they play. Here, two boys put down their rods and reels to catch more fishing bait.

Both sons and daughters of the oldest generation followed their fathers' example and married outside Shellcracker Haven, bringing new family members into the community to live. The next generation has done likewise, with a few exceptions. Now a fourth generation of children is growing up on the lake with toy rifles, trucks, **airboats, cast nets,** and dolls. If children become what they play, these toys are what the children of hunters and fishers will need if they are to reproduce the lifeways of their parents. Though children still represent the majority among the town's fishing families, their future appears to be one of diminishing opportunities.

MAKING A LIFE, MAKING A LIVING

What most houses in Shellcracker Haven have in common are boats and the pickup trucks used to pull them. Though they are not all the same kind, nor do they serve identical purposes, their presence shows the central role played by the lakes of the region in the lives and livelihoods of resident families today. Pickup trucks occupy an important position in the community, as they do in much of the Old South. They pull boats; haul equipment, supplies, hunting dogs, game, and children; and provide status and identity to the hunters and fishers who drive them.

Boats owned by the fishers and farmers of the older parts of town often serve commercial purposes. They are the tools of their owners' trades and are used to hunt alligators and to put out and take up **trotlines.** Men—and women, too, on occasion— seine "shiners," a popular baitfish. They gig frogs, hunt alligators, and guide sport hunters and recreational fishers.

Anyone in Shellcracker Haven will also tell you that boats are fun. Airboats fly over the surface of Shellcracker Lake, driven by huge, caged airplane propellers. Our

Jane W. Gibson

Mother and daughter enjoy the shade and each other's company as they rack fish boxes.

trailer sat on a narrow strip of land only a few yards from the lake on the west and a few yards from the train track on the east, so some days and nights were filled with engine noises. (This is my outsider's view, of course. Mr. Knight says he wakes up in the night if the scheduled train *doesn't* come through!) Other days appear slow and lazy, but that is the illusion given to those of us accustomed to separating work from play.

Work and social life flow seamlessly together in Shellcracker Haven. It is a life organized by hunting and fishing seasons mixed with occasional paid work in the bigger town nearby. These activities are not simply what people do for a living. They are central to identities as hunter and fisher families who work with great skill and knowledge, who must be self-disciplined, work hard and long when the time comes, and work together to pay the bills for their several households.

One day, after sending my husband and children off to other parts of the county for work and school, I set off on foot through the old lakefront neighborhood. As was often the case, women sat in their yards, talking and working in the shade of cypress and oak trees. They watched young children while baiting the handcrafted **fish boxes** their husbands, sons, and brothers would use for the night's fishing.

A fish box is actually a set of square, notched racks stacked on top of each other. The women, a mother and her married daughter, worked with what looked like tangled mounds of barbed fishing line piled into large metal tubs. They fed the sharp hooks, attached to the lines every few inches, into the notches of one rack before layering on the next rack to create the box. I asked about the problem of tangling, but they explained that for the most part, only beginners suffer with tangled lines; those with years of experience seldom have such problems. Once all the racks were lined

Jane W. Gibson

These little girls had been watching their grandmother rack a fish box, but they became more interested in the cleaning of last night's catch when I turned my camera in that direction.

with hooks, they were ready to be baited. Some fishermen prefer freshwater shrimp, but others swear by coral Lifebuoy soap.

That evening, men would load the baited boxes onto their boats and drive to favorite spots on one of several lakes in the region. Once in the water, one end of the fishing line would be secured to a stable post or limb. Then the boat would be driven across the area to be fished, reeling off the baited trotline into the water, one rack at a time, to the point at which the other end of the line would be secured. Laws require that trotlines be removed early in the morning, so after a night's rest, the fishermen would return to pull in whatever fish had taken the bait.

Early one day, I spotted a large crowd of children and a few grownups standing by a boat in front of a fisherman's home. As I drew near, I heard the sounds of admiration and awe for the enormous catfish on display. Some days fishermen get lucky. Some days they pull in lines of empty hooks. As the successful fisherman began cleaning his day's catch, his wife and mother began the process all over again, feeding hooked trotlines into racks with hope for that night's fishing.

Catfishing may be undertaken year-round by anyone with a license and the equipment. Mr. Knight's brother-in-law, Mr. King, acts as the local buyer because of his long-standing agreement with a commercial seafood business that sends a refrigerated truck to the community to buy processed catfish. Mr. King decides when and how many catfish he will buy from other families, and he buys from his own sons first. This means that those lower on the list must find buyers in grocery stores, seafood markets, or restaurants when they cannot sell their catfish in Shellcracker Haven.

Jane W. Gibson

The small building on the right is a cooler where alligators killed the night before await processing. To the left and just behind it is the skinning shed where the Knights spend many hours turning alligators into cubed fillets and raw hides.

Commercial fishing has long been a mainstay of the community, offering a reliable, though not lucrative, source of income for many families year-round, that is, within the limits of various buyers' willingness to purchase wild catfish. For this reason, the fishermen worry now because competition from farm-raised catfish has steadily reduced both demand and price paid to Shellcracker Haven fishing families.

I left the women baiting fish boxes and walked down the street and around a corner to Mr. and Mrs. Knight's house. Mr. Knight and his son built the skinning shed next to the house when they learned that alligator hunting with sales of meat and hides would become legal again. Boats and a walk-in cooler sit in the small yard in front of the shed. The shed is a small building, about 250 square feet, with walls, concrete floor, stainless steel tables, and equipment kept spotlessly clean. I learned that the family would meet early the next morning to process alligators brought in from the hunt. I happily accepted the invitation to join them.

At 7 A.M., I met the Knights at the skinning shed. Mrs. Knight turned on the fan in the corner and joined her daughter Elaine, daughter-in-law Anna, and nephew Owen at the table in the center of the room. Their job is to process the expensive white meat, removing membranes and gristle, and cutting it into filets. Red meat cannot be sold, so it goes into the freezer and is divided among family members. Mrs. Knight's son David waited for Mr. Knight and his son-in-law, Rodney, to bring in the first gator. David and the meat processors sharpened their knives, adding a rapid rhythmic sound, "kiska-kiska-kiska," to the sounds of a whirring fan and the confident chatter of people who have enacted the same scene many times.

Rodney and Mr. Knight entered, straining under the weight of a bull alligator that they carried to the stainless steel table on the back wall. Mr. Knight stretched a mea-

Jane W. Gibson

Mr. Knight scrubs the alligator to remove bacteria before the skinning begins.

suring tape from the snout to the tip of the tail and called out to David, "Eleven feet, three inches." David recorded the length and tag number in a ledger while Mr. Knight sprinkled the alligator with an abrasive disinfectant. After a thorough scrubbing on both sides, Mr. Knight hosed off the cleanser.

Referring to a photocopy of this hunt's skinning instructions, taped to an adjacent wall above a desk, Mr. Knight and Rodney made the first cuts, ringing the alligator's feet. They drew their knives up the outside of the legs to the back and located the position for tabs to appear on the hide. Rodney cut the prescribed pattern that would confirm that the hide had been processed legally. The two worked slowly and carefully, stopping often to sharpen their knives. Gradually, using short strokes, the skin was separated from the membrane that bound it to the alligator's body. With the valuable hide removed, the gator appeared naked, with only leather gloves and hood remaining on the head and feet.

Rodney and Mr. Knight transferred the carcass to the adjacent stainless steel table where Rodney began to remove the marketable white meat from the long, heavy tail. While Mr. Knight returned to the cooler for the next alligator, Rodney placed large slabs into a bucket from which Mrs. Knight withdrew pieces for those at her table to begin their work. Periodically, Anna and Elaine left the filleting process to tenderize, weigh, and package the meat for sale to a local restaurant. On every box, Anna recorded the alligator tag number, the weight of the meat, and the packaging date, all required by law.

The family worked with a rhythm and clearly defined division of labor in a "disassembly line" that revealed their experience with the tasks they carried out and with each other. Their efficiency filled the shed's two freezer chests with meat and the

Jane W. Gibson

Separating the hide from the body requires experience and patience.

cooler with hides that David would later preserve with salt. Alligator feet filled the sink and severed heads lined up like dominoes in the corner of the room. Anna, Elaine, and Mrs. Knight would sell these to a taxidermist who, in turn, would create back-scratchers, ashtrays, key chains, trophy skulls, and other kitsch that University of Florida "Fightin' Gator" fans like to display.

Outside, a cat purred loudly as it feasted on bits of meat left on an alligator skeleton. Nearby, in the bed of a newly arrived pickup truck, two biologists picked through alligator organs as part of their research. The Timex watch one found in a stomach gave rise to peels of laughter in the shed, and the predictable question: Was it still ticking? It was not.

With the results of their own and others' successes the night before, the Knights worked until late afternoon with only a short break for a sandwich at lunch. Mrs. Knight said she was worn out when the last hides and meat were finally out of sight, the paperwork was completed, and the room was sanitized for what they hoped would be another full day's work. The family earned the certificates displayed on gleaming white walls that demonstrate the state's agricultural and health departments' approval for meat processing. The day's work was behind them. They had enjoyed each other's company, laughing at each other's stories and jokes, sharing

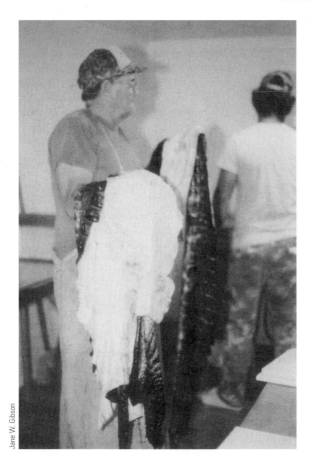

Mr. Knight holds the long hide draped over both arms. Later, someone will scrape off the bits of meat that still cling to it, salt it heavily, and roll it up for storage where it will remain until it is sold.

information, seeking and giving advice, and visiting with family and neighbors who stopped in to hear about the hunt.

AT THE END OF THE DAY

No one expects to get rich in Shellcracker Haven, but everyone eats, has a roof overhead, and stays warm on the occasional cold winter day. Most important to David, Mr. Knight's eldest son, is that he is master of his own life. He explains that he doesn't want a desk job that has him coming and going on someone else's schedule. He likes being his own boss, something he would have to give up if he worked for someone else.

Shellcracker Haven's families have created an economic system that has proven itself adaptive in its diversity and flexibility. True to his strong sense of pragmatism, Mr. Knight explained, "We do anything we can to make a living." What the people in this tiny community produce winds up in local, state, national, and international markets: highly prized alligator meat, the largest hides and most expensive alligator leather, hunting trophies, wild catfish, freshwater shrimp and other fishing bait, frog legs, turtle meat, artificial trees, boats, small craft items, honey, and fighting cocks.

Jane W. Gibson

Women cut large slabs of white meat into fillets.

In the midst of fast-paced, anything-for-a-buck Florida, the people of tiny Shellcracker Haven lead lives born in an earlier time period that has all but disappeared from the 21st-century American landscape. Here, commercial fishing and alligator hunting keep families close to each other through work and play as they have done for almost a century. As we'll see, however, both environmental and political factors condition all hunting and fishing activities, as well as the social world in which they are embedded.

2/Farming, Fishing, and Tapping the Turpentine

Unlike many rural North American communities, Shellcracker Haven has avoided demographic decline since the Great Depression. Some families stayed and grew, and some left as opportunities to work dried up. Those who remained adjusted to the changing conditions wrought by forces outside the town, shifting as needed and as possible among available livelihood strategies. According to local memories, never in its history did Shellcracker Haven families survive with only one kind of work, even when there was a clear identification with farming, fishing, or working the turpentine. Survival depended on hard work and social networks that crossed the boundaries of race and economic sectors, and combined flexibility with opportunism. Even today, though the community does not grow, it does not decline largely because of these characteristics. There are lessons to be learned here about sustaining families and communities.

The history of Shellcracker Haven that follows depends on a number of archival resources: 19th- and 20th-century census data, scholarly monographs on Florida history, county property records, and newspaper and popular magazine accounts. As a small, unincorporated village, whose importance to historians diminished relative to that of major cities, very little exists in writing about how it came to be as it is today. What do exist are the memories of elders in the town, some of these passed down from the earliest settlers. But memory is peculiar in its instability, and it is interesting because of its subjective qualities. Memories are remembered perceptions affected by many things: the passage of time, age, illness, storytelling, whether one grew up on a farm or on the lake, the qualities of individual experiences, and many other factors.

I had the pleasure of interviewing elders who experienced life on the farm, in the still quarters where black turpentine workers lived, on the lake, as laborers, and as children of small family business owners. I visited them in their homes, and in most cases I took along a video camera to record our conversations. The presence of a camera in an interview can be helpful, or it can be a hindrance, depending on the person being recorded. I was very lucky that those who gave me permission to tape seemed to enjoy the experience, and that the tapes have preserved words, facial expressions, body language, and both social and geographic context against the ravages of time.

Each person with whom I spoke carried a mental record that included the others, but their memories were not identical. All are situated in the text amidst information gathered elsewhere to provide the context for the experiences each person describes. I have included Mrs. Jameson's account of building the church. Her neighbors Bea and Morley talk about a variety of subjects: growing up on the farm, social life in the church, how farming related to turpentine production, and why farmers went out of business. Mr. Marshall spent his early years in the still quarters and tells about what life and work were like in the segregated community. Mabel reflects on the still quarters as a white outsider. Beth, who was the best friend of Mabel's sister, grew up in Shellcracker Haven. She tells about life on the lake and as the daughter of a successful commercial fisherman who invested in one of the two stores outside the turpentine commissary. Beth's father figured prominently as a mediator of early conflicts in the town. Sarah, who is Mabel's elderly mother, shows how cooperation between still quarters residents, fishermen, and Beth's family store helped all through the Great Depression.

19TH-CENTURY SETTLEMENT

They went singly, family by family, into the lands they cleared simply by accretion of farms into "neighborhoods." Their first communities were mere crossroads where scattered neighbors met. Their schools and churches and stores, like their camp meetings and their fairs, were set haphazardly in the open country or where roads met, with no ordered clustering and no fixed membership. . . .

In such communities, the settlers' unit of government, like their point of assemblage, was no town nor any fixed place. It was instead a rural "township" or several such diffuse authorities. It was not a single centering but instead a fluid crisscrossing net of emergent countrysides and cantons, variously linking farms in overlapping paths among spreading neighbors, kindred, and fellow-sectarians, about crossroad hamlets or open grounds of infrequent gathering. Even today in the Middle country, . . . this is the older community form in the countryside, and it persists among the farms despite the growth of towns, burgs, counties, and service centers, marks of later urban consolidation. . . .

Loose, open, kin based, . . . and subsistence farming rather than commercial- or urbanminded, . . . this culture and this community were a match. (Arensberg and Kimball 1965:110–11)

Shellcracker Haven arose from the bloody colonization of Florida by Spanish, French, British, and American armies, missionaries, and settlers. After "removal" of Native Americans in the infamous Seminole Wars, passage of the Armed Occupation Act of 1842 pushed remaining Seminole Indians south on the subtropical peninsula. This early homestead act placed the ancestors of today's Shellcracker Haven on the territorial frontier where, in exchange for land, they acted as a human buffer against Native American retaliation (Tebeau 1971).

With only soldiers' trails and wagon ruts to guide them, South Carolinian and Georgian descendants of Scottish, Irish, and German immigrants loaded horse- or mule-drawn wagons with children, furniture, and farm equipment. They made their way through sand hills, forests, marshes, and other unknown terrain to the cypress swamps and pine flat-woods surrounding Shellcracker Lake. Here the remote settlement grew slowly as a predominantly white community of subsistence farm families.

Early census records from the area give details today's government documents omit, partly because of laws concerning privacy, and partly because today's vast data sets would require enormous expenditure for such detail. I learned a great deal about individuals and families in the settlement: how many acres they owned, the names and ages of all the members of the household, the occupations of all working members, and property values. The 1850 census shows that four families, including the first **sharecropper** black family, constituted the entire settlement of 27 people. The Tomlinsons, ancestors of the Jamesons and two other families in residence today, and the Cramers, a family still found in Shellcracker Haven, were also among the first to arrive in the area (Murphy n.d.). Tomlinson, a Georgia farmer, homesteaded 60 acres that he, like other settlers to the basin, worked with the labor of his family. These small **yeoman farms,** clustered closely together in the Florida pine flat-woods near Shellcracker Lake, introduced a different settlement pattern into this part of the county. It contrasted markedly with the few large plantations worked by slaves before the Civil War.

Beginning before the Civil War and resuming at its end, investors and speculators pushed the railroad south. Among these was state Senator David Yulee, whose orange groves required a shipping line to ensure his profits. The Florida Internal Improvement Fund took the lead as seller of lands along the railroad, spurring population growth, local economic development, and inflation of lakefront property values. As an example, one lot in Shellcracker Haven changed hands five times in fifteen years.

The railroad built houses for its employees and, by 1879, extended its line to the lakeshore warehouse, dock, and turn track. The line soon ran through other lake communities, similarly settled by farmers, and connected larger towns to the north with Orlando, one of Florida's fastest-growing cities today. The small farm producers of Shellcracker Haven took advantage of their new market connections and added cash crops to subsistence production. Other industries grew up as well in the sales and shipping of milled timber, oranges, and fish seined from the lake.

A Mr. Wade made money on land speculation, and he owned and operated a steamboat named "Bessie" on Shellcracker Lake. The boat was 60 feet long by 25 to 30 feet wide, and Wade used it to haul oranges and vegetable produce across the lake in the winter. In warmer months, he sold moonlight rides to visitors and sightseers.

The train carried products to urban areas along the line and transferred some to a boat in Jacksonville to be shipped to Philadelphia, Boston, and New York. With such economic growth, opportunities to obtain wage labor jobs expanded, too. New and established farms needed help to weed and harvest vegetables, carry out these and other tasks in area orange groves, pack and load fish from the lake and locally grown produce, and harvest and mill local timber.

By 1880, the community's population reached 57, including two black sharecropping families. Five Knight households came from South Carolina to farm the fertile soils, fish the freshwater lake, and hunt the diverse and abundant game of Shellcracker Basin. By 1895, increased population and earnings stimulated by the railroad paid for a post office, a schoolteacher, three churches (a Baptist one for black families and Methodist and Baptist churches for white families), and three cemeteries.

Land changed hands frequently, driving up its price.

BUILDING A CHURCH, BUILDING COMMUNITY

In 1882, the Methodist church began its monthly meetings in a log cabin that doubled as a school, and then moved to the Baptist church where worship continued until 1898. That year, the Ewing family donated the land where the Methodist church sits today. Elderly residents can name their ancestors who milled the cypress cut from the area, constructed the building, made the pews by hand, and did the "fancy work" on the inside. The church is a physical symbol of their history in this place, one that ties them to each other and to the natural world. As argued by White (1967), the Bible separates the natural world from the human one and claims that God created the natural world for the benefit of people.

Every year, the church holds a homecoming celebration and invites all who have moved away to return for a worship service, music, and a meal. I attended a homecoming on the 107th anniversary of the church, one of many Sundays I spent there, and witnessed the continuation of the process whereby the building would embody the community. Suzanne, daughter of Sarah, made the stained-glass windows, each of which was dedicated at that homecoming to different church families. Two memorial dedications—the pavilion, where we would later enjoy lunch, and a set of offering plates and communion set—also marked the church as an expression of the community's present and past.

Mrs. Jameson, born in Shellcracker Haven in 1905, talked with me inside the church.

> It was 1882 when the church was organized, and they met at different places to have worship. One was the old log schoolhouse where all the children went to school, which is

Jane W. Gibson

The Methodist church was built with local hands, using wood cut and milled on the lake.

quite a ways down by the lake. But it was kind of the center of the community. Then when we all left the school, the church stopped going to the schoolhouse. They met around in the homes and they finally went to the Baptist church, the old-timey Baptist church that was up on the hill from the cemetery. From that, then—why, they went around until they decided to build the original church where we had services, so that was built way back before I was born.

It really started maybe in 1898, or maybe before that. And so it was built by the different ones in the community, and everybody that could have volunteered their work. And the lumber for the building was cut by a sawmill which was down by the lake. They got all that lumber as reasonable as they could. I understand quite a bit of the stuff was donated for the church.

My grandfather—he was yet living, and he worked to build the church—and my uncle Glen, they was two of the oldest ones. And then there was another gentleman, Mr. Joe Hayman, in charge of the turpentine, and I understand he had full charge of having our pews fixed. They was handmade and the rail around the altar, it was handmade. I think they was in connection with the mill and they had places where it was planed and machines that was good enough to do the fancy work.

This probably is the third roof anyway. The first roof, it was just like all the other material for the church. It was homemade cypress shingles. As everyone can see, the roof is very steep. Them old-timers got up there and fixed them shingles and had a ridging, a board on top of them. But they give way. The fishermen come out. Directly back of the church was thick oaks. And they poured out their fish heads and the buzzards got on the roof and tore the roof up.

Different people had big trees, timber you know, and the sawmill sawed it. And the old-timey ceiling that's in the church, that fancy ceiling with the beading you know, and it's put up perfect. We still have it. The lady down at Shellcracker Haven station, her husband was the agent for the depot, so she sold ice cream to the folks that come to ship the vegetables to help buy the piano. So we put a piano in, in the '20s. It was maybe '22. Suzanne did the stained-glass windows and the pad all around the altar. The organ was donated to us last year.

Like I say, we didn't ever own a car, but my father had a wagon, and we was all loaded in the wagon to come to church here. My first recollection, I can even remember my grandfather in this church. He wasn't very tall and he wore a derby. He had great big blue eyes and I can remember him sitting over in the pews on the south side of the church. I can remember my old Uncle Glen. He was superintendent of the Sunday school. We had old-timey kitchen chairs that went in the pulpit. Uncle Glen would get one of them chairs and sit right out front. We had songs and all, and one of them would be saying, "Well, it's time to go to classes." They would hold a bunch of the classes inside and outside maybe.

When I was in my teens—I was thirteen, I believe, when I started playing—and it was an old-timey pump organ situated by the railing. And you really had to work to get the sound, so I learned to play that while the old-timers were just singing the hymns. I learned to chord along, and later on I took a whole amount of twelve music lessons, and that's as far as I ever did get. I have a natural ear for music.

When they took the old organ out, a piano was put in, and I played the piano off and on. There was different younger girls that could play, but they had to go on to school or get work, and then I'd play again. They figured it up, and I've been playing about seventy years for this church.

So we have a great time out there at the church. From my childhood on I remember the church because my mother and father—there was quite a family of us—and we always went to church.

The church sat at the center of social life for Bea and Morley, who are some fifteen to twenty years younger than Mrs. Jameson.

JG: What did you do for fun?

Morley: Oh, that's the good part about it. We attended the Methodist church here, also the Baptist church. My family was Baptist, and we were brought up in both churches because my dad had some close friends that were Methodist, and when he was a boy, he would go to Sunday school at the Baptist church one Sunday and Methodist the next. Baptist church was out toward the cemetery, a quarter mile this side. There was a school back there, near the Potters' place. What I got is what Dad and Mother told me. It was a long building, one-room school, and the church used it for church services. Let me tell you, when we were teenagers coming up, we had socials at the church, like a chicken supper or boiled peanuts or a fish fry.

Bea: Everybody attended.

Morley: About once a month, we'd have something for the youth, and it was a lot of fun. We'd go from one neighbor to the next. Mrs. Jameson's mother and father, we'd have something over there, something at Mrs. Jameson's one time. My dad and a fellow from Shellcracker Haven barbecued a pig. Sat up all night barbecuing that pig. About noon the next day, it was ready to eat. In an open pit, cooked it real slow. Now that was good eating. The wood that was used seasoned the meat. Hickory.

Bea: Back then, it didn't take as much to live as it does now. I know it.

Jane W. Gibson

Then and now, the church brings people in the community together. These children are playing "red rover" at vacation Bible school.

Morley: Well, people in Shellcracker Haven, most are retired and on limited income, and those that are not are working like mischief to make ends meet, make their bills, and we don't have a cash flow like that to support it.

Mrs. Jameson married Oliver in the church over eighty years ago at the age of sixteen. They and many others brought their babies there to be baptized, and many now lie in the church cemetery. I walked among the tombstones with Mrs. Jameson as she pointed out the graves belonging to her family.

> That's the community part over there, and over this way is my family. My aunts and uncles are in this area here. My Aunt Blanche is buried here. Aunt Maude is buried there. They were my mother's sisters. Her first daughter, Madge, is buried where this bush is. Here is my mother and father's graves, and this is my sister.
>
> I was five years old when my grandfather passed away. I remember my mother. We loaded up when we had his funeral, and we took this long ride to the cemetery in the horse and wagon. We passed this old-timey field, and there was a little log smokehouse where my Grandma Cramer lived. The crepe myrtles was in bloom. It was the only mark left of my grandmother.

Virtually everyone has someone buried in the local white cemetery. Mrs. Knight's little five-year-old sister lies among other family members. The little girl fell and hit her head on the railroad tracks that ran beside her house, and the doctor misdiagnosed the injury. Mrs. Knight says their family never really recovered after she died. Now her mother and father are there, too.

The "Potter patch" occupies a corner of the cemetery. Here Mr. Potter, who is Mrs. Jameson's cousin, buried his parents, grandparents, and, only a few years ago,

Jane W. Gibson

The white cemetery

his son who was killed in a helicopter crash. Morley buried his father and grandfather there, and he and Bea expect to join them someday.

REMEMBERING FARM LIFE

We didn't have telephones, electric lights, TVs, anything back then, you know. We loved it! We got along good!

Bea, April 1986

On a hot, dry April day, I drove down the graded county road, throwing up yellow dust clouds as I passed sun-baked pastures. Soon I arrived at Morley's and Bea's house to keep our appointment for a videotaped interview about their families' histories in Shellcracker Haven. The community I had found to be "closed" eight months earlier had become warm and generous in ways I'd experienced only from family and close friends. As we talked, an oscillating fan provided welcome relief from the oppressive Florida heat.

Morley's wife, Bea, is Mr. Knight's niece. She knows little of her family history except that her father was born in Shellcracker Haven. Morley's grandfather homesteaded land very near the county line. Morley's father—Mr. Harry, he was called, showing both affection and respect—bought an additional hundred acres, "not all of it under cultivation, a lot of it still raw woods," near the original homestead.

JG: Bea, tell me about growing up here.

Bea: I was born and raised here, so it just seems like home to me. I wouldn't be happy nowhere else. Daddy had 80 acres here and all his kids are living on that but two. Mostly I had the ten kids while Mama worked on the farm. I was the housekeeper and baby-tender. We'd take the babies to the field and put the quilt to lay the babies on, and I had to keep the babies on that quilt, which wasn't too hard to do then because I guess they'd mind or something. It was no trouble. Mama had them; I tended to them. Done the cooking and housecleaning. And Daddy worked at the turpentine still, too. He made the barrels for the rosin.

Morley: [Bea's dad] was a guy that didn't back up from any job. He would do it some way. He had a lot of ego. He wanted to go forward. He wanted to have something. He worked awful hard. The children worked, too. They could grumble, complain, but it didn't make any [difference]. He'd say, "Get it, just get it."

Bea: He worked hard all his life. He used to work all day long at the still and come home, and we'd have to go out in the woods and saw down pine trees and bring them up. We stacked it for Daddy and helped him split it. People back then had woodstoves and had to have wood. Got a dollar and a quarter a strand. That was a pile of wood!

Morley: It was 4 foot high, 8 foot long, and the logs are 2 foot across. It's a lot of work. But my goodness, you could buy groceries! I bet you his grocery bill was four or five dollars a week.

Bea: Probably.

Morley: Most of it, a big part of it, was on the farm. You didn't have to buy any bacon.

Bea: No syrup, no vegetables, no milk.

JG: You made your own syrup? Tell me about that.

Morley: An open kettle. It's built with a furnace, had a boiler, 80 gallons. Eighty gallons of cane juice, fill that up. Had your own mill. Grind your own cane out, and you boil it. And out of 80 gallons of juice, you'd get about 8 gallons of syrup.

Bea: It'd take a long, long time to cook that off, though.

Morley: You could start real early, four o'clock in the morning, sometimes five, get a boiling on. While you were boiling that one out, you'd grind up another one. And by doing that, you could get three or four a day.

JG: Did you grow your own sugar cane?

Bea: Mm-hmm.

Morley: This year's crop, you cut it off at the ground. Next year, it puts on a shoot, puts on more. Keep it cut off. Every third or fourth year, plow it out, take the top, and plant that.

Bea: I remember chewing a lot of it.

Morley: Even made candy out of it. Boil it down real thick, and pull it and pull it, and it would turn white. Pull it a little bit more and you'd have it. Be hard as a brick. We had a birthday party over here, and we had a candy pulling. That was part of the program. We had a birthday cake, and you had a prize. You know what it was? A nickel baked in that cake!

JG: What about your family, Morley? When did they come here?

Morley: My parents were raised here. They was born and raised right here, out in the country about three miles from the post office.

JG: Is your father the famous Mr. Harry?

Morley: That's the name! He was a farmer. We had the farm, and the boys took care of the cattle, hogs, and horses, whatever, and he lived here all of his life with the exception of a year or two, something like that. Did a lot of fishing on the lake. When it was time to farm, we stayed on the farm. This time of year, we farmed our cash crops. Then we'd go fishing to supplement our income with catfish.

In my interviews with community residents, it was common for them to distinguish, as Morley does, between "people in Shellcracker Haven" and the farmers in the community. Farmers thought of themselves as living outside the business center of the village around which clustered the houses of former railroad employees and fishermen. As we'll see, the semantic distinction does not reflect the fact that farmers fished and fishing families had gardens, nor does it indicate the interdependence, the intermarriages, or the shared social life of the two "sides." Morley continues:

Morley: With the people in Shellcracker Haven, they were either farmers *or* fishermen, and that's the way they were brought up, where my dad was a farmer *and* a fisherman. Well, my grandfather was a farmer *and* a fisherman. Course when he was fishing a hundred years ago, possibly, he shipped his fish himself. In barrels, they shipped fish from [the depot]. It was legal to catch game fish, ice them down, and ship them from there.

My dad wholesaled fish here at Shellcracker Haven and delivered them. He had a regular route that he went on, possibly in the late '20s. He bought fish here from the **fish house** and then sold them, and he also fished. He stayed busy. He had to. We had five children besides my grandparents and my oldest half brother. Made six children.

JG: Everybody worked?

Morley: Oh yeah, and in the summertime, it was awful out there for a boy, warm weather. Always happy when the cloud come up, cover the sun, make a little breeze.

JG: What other responsibilities did you have?

Bea: Mine was mostly taking care of the children. I had to get the fodder, get the corn, and we had to cut okra in the muck down there. But mostly I tended the children. I didn't do much farm work. That's the reason, so Mama could work in the fields, work with the hoe and gather the crops. It was a hard job.

JG: Did the children also help on the farm?

Bea: Oh yeah, once they got big enough, mostly gathering like the corn, potatoes, and vegetables. Kids are different now. We give them too much now. Anything they want they go to the store and get. Give instead of earn it.

JG: When you had treats, did you have to earn that money?

Bea: [laughs] I don't remember having any treats really. We had kids to survive on the farm. We didn't have luxuries like they have now. We didn't have telephones, electric lights, TVs, anything back then, you know. We loved it! We got along good! I always had food: bacon, pork. We had a smokehouse, always had meat in it. Always had vegetables. Always had milk.

JG: What kinds of things did you need cash for?

Bea: Not too much food. Coffee and flour.

Morley: Sugar.

Bea: Sugar and rice and corn. We'd take our corn to [the next town] and have it ground for grits and meal. We didn't have a car. It was years later when Daddy finally got a car. It was a 1932 Chevrolet. It wasn't new. He went up the dirt road. We had a horse and wagon.

Morley: We didn't have a highway back then. You could go from Shellcracker Haven on a single rut road through the woods.

Farming seemed to place such demands on everyone's time that I wondered where education might fit in.

JG: What about schools in the area?

Morley: We went to school. We had to attend. It was state law. If you missed very many days, the lady was out to see why. It isn't like it is now. They couldn't do much about it, but they could sure come out and talk to you. Make you think they were going to do something. Most of us at our age wanted to go to school.

Bea: Right.

Morley: Had a desire, because if you stayed home, there was work that had to be done. And people had a desire to go, see, anyway through elementary school. There was quite a dropout in high school. Kids would get large enough where they could go out and get a job, and they thought they had it made. Still, today, they drop out.

The only time we had work was during the summer between school terms. We got a chance to do some work in harvesting. Out here, we harvested vegetables.

My first two years in school was right behind the house here. It was a two-room school, wooden building, and we didn't need but one. We didn't have that many students. In my class, there was four in second grade, first and second, and they only taught up to the eighth grade. And if they went to [high] school, they had to go to [the next town]. At one time, they had a bus going up there, but it got to where they didn't have enough children to pay a bus, and in the '30s, it was hard to go to school. They needed to pick up what work they could do to get money to help support the family during the Depression. I wasn't old enough then to have any responsibility other than what we had at home, which was enough, I thought. I was about twelve or thirteen.

Bea: I went to the seventh grade. I finished after the war. Morley and I both finished at night classes. Well, something you want to do—get that high school diploma.

Morley: I got it, but what good was it? I was too old to advance in my work, and there was no advancement. But the only thing is, I got my high school diploma. I can say I went through high school.

Mr. Harry and Bea's father, like other farmers in the area, grew cotton, corn, lima beans, snap peas, okra, cucumbers, potatoes, and sometimes watermelon. What they did not sell or eat, women canned to sell locally and to provide vegetables to their families through the winter. Given their reliance on their own muscles and such simple technologies as a horse- or mule-drawn plow, it was clear they would need more workers than even a large family could supply. Nor was food from the farm all the food that families needed or wanted. The interdependence of the community now becomes apparent, expressed most clearly with reference to the Great Depression.

JG: All those crops require a lot of hands. Was labor a problem?

Morley: We had a turpentine still over here and a lot of colored people, and that's where we'd get our labor. When it comes time for the harvesting, like lima beans, snap beans, squash, whatever, [we] had plenty of labor.

JG: How did the Depression affect your families?

Bea: I remember we used to trade eggs or chickens for insurance. We hardly ever give money. Mrs. Peck used to always bring us material, something to make our school clothes out of. Probably gave them vegetables or syrup, something like that. You helped everybody out then, you know. You didn't think nothing about giving everybody a ham or a chicken.

Morley: I got one story. We needed a roof on our house. Mrs. Jameson's husband came over to help my daddy put it on. They must have worked two or three days putting the roof on that house, two days at least. They got finished. Why, Daddy wanted to pay him. He said, "No, you can't pay me. This is a neighborly deed." That's the kind of neighbors we had back then. So in the fall of the year, Daddy loaded him up two pigs, pretty good size, carried them over, gave them to him, said, "That's for putting the roof on my house." So they butchered them, had pork. I was just a teenager. I remember that, and now it's always stuck with me—a neighborly deed. Money isn't everything.

I think we were very fortunate here. We had small farms and we could grow food. We had the lake down there. You could catch fish. And at that time you could sell game fish. It was hard on some. There was no money involvement. But on the farm, we had produce we could exchange and what have you. We did a lot of exchanging out here with the colored people. They'd come down to buy stuff off the farm. If they didn't have money, they'd get a five-pound bag of sugar out of the commissary, the company store, and we traded, see?

Following is another view of community integration through barter and reciprocity, as expressed by Emmett, a black city commissioner for some twenty years in a town near Shellcracker Haven. Emmett was born in the still quarters in the early 20th century and lived there for many years. Here are Emmet's words:

In the evening, they [mothers] was in the bean fields picking beans for the white peoples who had the big fields, as we called it.

Quite naturally you carried your children because that was more money for the family coming in, doing cucumbers and lettuce and squash and stuff like that. They was getting 50 cents a day, but they had to pay a dime of that to ride. So really they was getting 40 cents. This was not a company truck. This was a private one. Children made 25 cents or 30 cents a day.

At the time, the people was close, even though we was segregated, but the white people we could go and buy milk. And some of them would even give you some because they had more than they needed for their family. Some families you could trade eggs or maybe sweet potatoes for milk. You didn't do a whole lot of buying back then because the money wasn't available. Didn't nobody have no money. So there was a lot of swapping.

There wasn't too much hunting. The mens were working all the time in the turpentine, so if they ran across a rabbit or a turtle, they'd kill it right then while they was working. But there wasn't a lot of hunting like there is now. It wasn't enough time. Back then you didn't find too many peoples had a gun in their house. Wasn't that much hunting to do. Just a very few people that might have a shotgun.

Out there at the quarters there wasn't no time for fishing. I can remember parents would send out to Shellcracker Haven if the truck didn't come through. Back then those people would give us the catfish heads, and we would make stew. That's the way we lived. They would sell the catfish. Some of them, they would give us. That's what a lot of black families lived off of. We ate catfish stew. We strived on that.

Farms failed, and abandoned homesteads were eventually torn down.

While the Depression did much to promote community integration, the changing structure of agriculture across the country and in Florida was making farming an increasingly difficult way to make a living, especially for those with small farms.

JG: What happened to farming?

Morley: I really don't know. Well, I'll tell you one thing, and I guess that's the main thing. It got to where when you grew something, you couldn't sell it. Big companies with large acreage took the market from smaller farms.

Bea: Well, the price was too low.

Morley: Well, we had buyers, and still have them. See, if you grow something, you got to haul it clear down there and let them sell it for you. Used to, we'd haul it here to [the depot in Shellcracker Haven], stamp it. We had a stamp for a commission house in New York, Boston, wherever, and we'd ship there. Most were shipped to New York or Philadelphia, some to other states, too.

We wasn't a big enough operation to pay off. During the Depression, the farmers had to increase their acreage, and if you couldn't afford to increase your acreage, you couldn't make a living anymore, so you had to get out and work. Anyone that could afford it enlarged the farm by renting or buying more property. It finally got to where that didn't pay off.

JG: How big would you have to have been?

Morley: Well now, used to, when I was a kid, a 40-acre farm was all one family would need. What could you do? You grew a cash crop like your beans, okra, and when that was off, you'd plant it with corn, peanuts for your livestock. You didn't need a big farm. But later on, why, if you didn't have a tractor, with all the equipment and a hundred or so acres,

A few cows are about all that's left of farm life in Shellcracker Haven.

you wasn't a farmer anymore. Normally, you had a two-horse farm; two horses or two mules would take care of it. A 50- or 60-acre farm, or maybe 60 to 80 acres.

Whether it was the companies or whatever that took it over, see, the growing of the crops, if you grew something now, you have to carry it to a produce broker. He makes a sale, he gets a commission, and you don't know who else gets one before it gets back to the grocery store. It's the only way you could sell.

Bea: Yeah. Farmer always does the work. Somebody else gets the money.

JG: Were any families from here able to enlarge their farms?

Morley: Yeah, I had an uncle and a cousin that enlarged their farm, and the family over here [points to the south], they bought more land. The family was related to my daddy. Sort of distant.

JG: Why did they quit?

Morley: It got to where they couldn't make anything, and they got disabled and the children didn't take over. Same thing happened with the [uncle and cousin]. As long as they were able, they farmed. They got disabled, they had to quit. We had a small farm. My daddy had a hundred acres. Not all of it was under cultivation. A lot was still raw woods. My dad sold their place to his sister, and they cleared a lot of land. And we bought 20 acres adjoining them, and we cleared a third of it ourselves and put it in cow pasture. We still have cows. We got some cows here and some over there. It's all in the family.

REMEMBERING THE STILL QUARTERS

Toward the end of the 17th century, the increased costs of shipping Swedish turpentine products moved the British government to encourage turpentine production in the colonies. After its settlement in 1665, North Carolina became the center of the

naval stores industry, the business that got its name from the uses of its products for caulking wooden ships and for preservative treatment of their rigging (Hill 1950).

Turpentine businesses followed the pine trees south and west into Georgia and north Florida, and though no one knows precisely when the woods around Shell-cracker Haven became important to turpentine producers, by the late 1880s, turpentine was distilled in the community. Here, the line drawn between slaves and whites in the south before 1865, was drawn around the still quarters after emancipation. At least six adult men from the community had fought for the Confederacy during the Civil War. Except for Morley's grandfather, they returned safely to the community, to farming and raising families in a world that still clings to a belief in white racial superiority.

I met Emmett at his house in the town to which he migrated after leaving work in the turpentine industry. He gave me almost four hours of his day and told me about the life of black turpentiners. I asked him, "What does a turpentiner do?" Here is his answer:

It was a strenuous job, sun up to sun down, maybe half a day on Saturday, and not at all on Sunday. There was chipping the boxes, put the scrapes on it to make the turpentine run out. When they got a certain height, they called it pulling boxes. So they was getting cents per hundred. Turpentine was probably 50 or 75 cents a barrel. A good worker might get two barrels a day, I guess. So they didn't make a whole lot of money.

Most of them had mule and wagon, and, depending on how far they had to go, the truck would take them. The trucks had skids, two long poles. Once you got a barrel full—most of the time it was more than one person, or sometimes it was a family if you had enough children—you'd gather them and you might have four or five barrels. You put them off in the woods, and the truck driver would go from job to job. He had skids, and we would roll that barrel up on the truck and the truck would carry the barrel back to the still.

I can remember I was too small to see the woods rider who ran the commissary, too. When I got big enough to remember, Mr. Samuels was the woods rider. In any quarters, Phifer or Campville, they had a woods rider who was also responsible for the commissary.

The same company owned all three turpentine operations. The woods rider was the white overseer for the company that owned most of the trees but leased some from local landowners. Emmett continues:

Still was right off from the commissary. I had an uncle that worked out at the still. They made the barrels. There was wooden slats and steel bands. They put them together. They made the lids and everything

When they paid off once a month, then the company would let the truck bring the peoples to [the next town]. That was to get their dry goods or clothing, or if they wanted anything besides the chicken they had on their yard. It was **jukes** back then, but see, me being young, I wasn't even allowed close to them. We didn't have too many of the adults that hung around the jukes because you either got on the truck when the time was up or you walked back that night.

We as children, only thing we had was getting out there in the road in the evening, and there wasn't a whole lot of that. Maybe once a week if they'd gather at somebody's house, mostly Friday and Saturday, and they'd get the rosin, what they done cooked all the turpentine out, and have a fire in somebody's yard.

The "rolling store" come through the quarters once a week. A little extra money could buy things the commissary didn't have: soda water, 5 cents orange crush, Hires root beer, candy, cookies. Back then, everybody worked. When a child got big enough in that family, in order to make ends meet, he had to work. And I still tell people, then was the good old bad times.

The company was owned by an influential family in the county and run by local white men who oversaw the work of black laborers. One man described the status of these jobs as such that no white men would have them, though some of the tasks resemble those performed today by forest resource managers. The ground around the pine trees had to be cleared of brush to protect the trees from both natural and managed fires. Workers then "chipped" the trees, placed a metal tap and cup against the wound, and later returned in mule- or horse-drawn wagons to scrape the sap into the large wooden barrels Bea's father made for a time. Rosin was then transported to the still where it was heated by a wood fire, and the distillation process yielded turpentine and other products that were discarded. As Morley described it:

> This was a big furnace. It had a large kettle, sealed. It was bricked over, and at the top it had an opening where they'd pour in raw gum into the kettle. And when they had so many barrels, they would cap it and build a fire under it. And the way they got spirits of turpentine was through evaporation. After it got cooked out, as much minerals and spirits as they could, then they had a vat and they had a strainer on it, and they put batting in; and when it got down so low, they'd turn that cooked gum out into that vat. The batting would filter the impurities out—chips and wood and metal—and it would be a clear liquid. Then when it dripped out so much, they would take the strainer off the vat, and they dipped it and poured it into the barrels that he made. Then they had a cap inside of them. When they got those things filled, they'd roll them out in the field and after so many days, they go out there and pull the caps out to see if the rosin had set up. Then the truck came in and loaded it for Jacksonville.

Black families lived in the quarters located about half way between the white farmers' lands and the lake community of commercial fishers. By the time of the Great Depression, the quarters inside Shellcracker Haven consisted of seventy-five to one hundred houses, according to Emmet.

JG: What were the still quarters like?

Emmett: I call them the shotgun houses, long, with really straight halls. Wasn't no partitions; well, some of them did. With just a tin top, with no ceiling like that [pointing to the textured ceiling above us]. Some of them's in such bad shape when you were laying out at night—what we called it, "looking at the stars." When it rained, we put the pots and pans out to catch the water to keep the bed [dry], or maybe you move the bed wherever we could.

To me at that time, they was bad condition, and yet they was good. We didn't have to pay no rent. Just so long as somebody was working for the company, you could stay in the house.

They were regular common wood houses. Most of them had fireplaces. We had a woodstove.

JG: Did the company provide the stove?

Emmett: Everybody had to get their own. The company didn't furnish nothing but the house. One family to a house. You might have four or five children sleeping in one bed or pads on the floor. Wasn't no toilets at that time. We had outhouses. I don't think all of the houses even had that. Some houses would share; some had one for themselves. A lot of peoples even went out to the woods.

There wasn't no running water. In the quarters of Shellcracker Haven, if I can remember right, there was two pumps or maybe three pumps serving the entire quarters.

Mabel came with her parents to Shellcracker Haven some sixty-five years ago. She is a white woman and the daughter of one of the town's earliest commercial fishers. She remembers the still quarters from a distance:

> I don't believe you'd ever find a more primitive industry or a more primitive people or more primitive conditions. They had very little to eat, and not even enough of that, and a lot of the women would hire out to do menial jobs, whatever they could do. They would walk from the turpentine still, which is, I guess, three miles from the still to here. Laundry, housework was about all that was available here, but that was a means of survival.
>
> To me, primitive as I saw it and they were living at that time, the only thing they had was dipping the gum and chipping the trees, and it was always for the company. And of course there was very little money in it, and they always had large families. Yeah, they had no birth control. I had eleven. Their homes were more or less huts, and in order to keep themselves warm, they had to seal the inside of it with some kind of paper, the Sears and Roebuck catalog or some kind of paper using paste and water. They had a commissary, but they charged such exorbitant prices for the food that the little bit of money that they made just would not go anywhere.

Emmett's story suggests that the farming and turpentining communities had more in common than just large families. At the time of my interview, I didn't know yet that rural electrification would extend to Shellcracker Haven after the still quarters closed down. Thus, all shared the conditions of rural isolation, and all adapted with subsistence production.

JG: Did you have electricity or refrigeration in the quarters?

Emmett: No. I can remember that we used to dig a hole in the ground, like if we had fresh meat. Dig a hole, get sawdust, put that down in the ground. Then you wrapped whatever meat you had, which we didn't have that much meat, maybe a chicken or sometimes they'd kill a hog. Wrap it in newspaper and put it down in the ground. And that's the way they kept it. Pack it in sawdust and "crocusite," and that's the way we did it. And it did work.

Most every house had a little garden. It wasn't that much room for each house, so it was a real small garden. You might have a little okra or greens. The main thing everybody had was sweet potatoes, and when you gathered those and you were back in the smokehouse, you'd lay them down in pine straw and they would keep. That's how we kept them.

Most families had one or two hogs, a chicken, and I can't think of but one black family that had a cow, or maybe a couple of cows, but most of them raised their own meat and their own vegetables. And I can remember they had the smokehouse when you killed a hog. The other peoples out there killed their own meat. They didn't have to carry it nowhere like they do now. You had your own smokehouse in your own backyard.

When we had sweet potatoes and you killed a hog in the winter and cured the meat, you had enough meat to last you. If you plant enough sweet potatoes and bed them down in pine straw, they would last you. The ladies did a lot of canning okra, tomatoes, beans, peas. Whatever they growed, they canned. So when the crop was gone, they still had stuff that came in from the smokehouse.

Living in the middle of a white community that believed in its own God-given right to subordinate blacks meant that blacks had to know and keep "their place." Emmett remembers how strict, internal discipline was transmitted to black children by their families and community members. I wondered at the ferocity of that discipline: Could it have been partly explained by the needs of adults to vent feelings about unjust treatment? Here are Emmett's comments:

Just about every house in the quarters had a little fence around it with a gate, and just about every one of them had a cowbell on that gate, so when somebody come in they knew somebody was coming in.

With all the cracks in the house, whether it was in the floor or the ceiling or the walls, we used to have to pad up the wall with cardboard and whatnot. But anyhow, we'd be wishing for somebody to come to the house so we'd get a chance to go out to the back. And I'll never forget this time. Miss Caroline Ramsey came to the house, and they was sitting on the porch. When the bell on that gate rang, we knew to go out back, and we was wanting that anyway so we could go out slip on across the woods. But we stayed to where we could see, cause when Mama called us we were in hearing distance—but this particular time, we was inside the house. And if a young lady got pregnant, it was hid. We didn't know it. And that conversation was not out in the street like it is today. When I grew up, you didn't see above a woman's ankles. They wore the long dresses.

Anyhow, we going to get smart cause all the houses way up off the ground. We goes around back like we was playing, crawl all the way up under the house. He was short. He could almost stand up. That's how high the houses were. We were going to peek through the crack to hear what they was talking about cause we'd gotten word that somebody got pregnant in the quarters and we thought we was going to be able to hear. Miss Caroline spotted us, and she had snuff in her mouth. The women dipped snuff. Miss Caroline spit right through that crack in my eyes, and my grandmother got my cousin eyes, and then we still got a whipping.

It's not like today, with children sitting around with parents or with any adults and listen to their conversation. We couldn't do that. If an adult came to the house to see my grandmother or my grandfather, we didn't sit in their presence. That was the rule. You did not listen.

We was really disciplined back then, and any adults could discipline you. I can remember getting a whipping by other families more than my own grandmother. If you were in the quarters playing and did something wrong, you'd get a whipping, and they'd tell your parents and you got another whipping. I guess this is one of the reasons I don't care for meat skin. I got three whippings one time about meat skin.

When she called me, I knew to go. Any child knew to go when an adult called them. And she had me to go on the back porch where her husband. And see, back then they didn't whip you with your clothes on because they made them and they'd tell you they was not going to wear those clothes out whipping you.

Emmett and other children from the quarters attended a segregated school, though Emmett's own attendance was reluctant. In his words:

School was a little white building right off from the church. Kids walked there about a mile. Back then, one teacher taught whatever. My first teacher was from the quarters. One teacher and one room. There wasn't too many older kids went to school. I pretty well educated myself. "Mother wit" they call it. The little bit of teaching I got back then, I wasn't crazy about it, but I had to go. I think about it now.

We didn't have too many good books. They was handed down from some of the white children. Our parents had to furnish pen and pencil and paper. That was some of the things that come out of the commissary, the brown pen and pencil. The paper looked like recycled paper today.

In spite of beliefs that kept the two communities racially segregated, in residents' minds, if not in their behaviors, the white community took some responsibility for black children's education. Not only did books come from the white school, but Morley and Bea told me how members of the white community supplied a school building.

Bea: My daddy helped do it. I remember the log rolling. A mule was pulling it, and kids were behind that building watching it. It was interesting. They had to clear the road out for it, cut bushes, trees. Had to be a long time cause there's a mile across there. I remember having to help move those logs.

Morley: They picked the logs up from behind the building and put it in front. This was a better building than the one the colored people had, a larger building and a better building, and then after they closed the colored school here, they moved that school to [the next town]. Probably by that time it was on a truck.

And just as the church played a vital role in the social life of the white community, the black church and its cemetery did the same for residents of the still quarters. Bea remembered that her father had built caskets for the black community's deceased, and she remembers them as mostly baby caskets.

Emmett: Everybody's striving to go to church. We had to walk about a mile and a half to church. The church wasn't in the quarters. It was down the road. . . . Wednesday night, everybody went to prayer meeting. I doubt if you'd find three families left in the quarters Wednesday night. Then on Sunday morning, you'd see the crowd going back down the same road. The girls was just like the boys. We only had the one pair of dress shoes and wore them on Sunday. Through the week we didn't wear them shoes to school. We went barefooted even if it was cold. You see, everybody—we pulled off those shoes when we got to church, and just as we get out of the churchyard, everybody put those shoes back on.

JG: What denomination was the church?

Emmett: It was a Baptist church. Grove Baptist Church. Certain families still bury out there. Some of them grew up out there. The one buried out there Saturday wasn't born and raised out there, but they still have ties because his grandmother and parents were buried there.

Usually on Sunday morning, somebody would ring the bell so you'd know it was time to go to church, and in the quarters, as far as it was, if somebody died, somebody got to that church. They walked up there and what we called "toning the bell" that somebody died. The telephone tells everybody now. It was a signal, and everybody was close-knitted and everybody did whatever it was to be done. In other words, everybody in the quarters was just totally one family even if they wasn't related by blood.

I can remember if somebody got sick, if a woman got sick, the women in the quarters did whatever that woman was supposed to do in that house: cook, wash clothes, iron, clean. If a man got sick, then the mens of the quarters did that man's chores. He didn't have no income if he was sick, so the men would share what they had. If he needed wood, cause everybody was heating by wood, everybody would bring wood, and either the adults or children would cut it up and stack it in the corner.

We had a midwife, and if there was any medical complications, Dr. Floyd, he was the only doctor in the whole eastern part of the county at that time. My great-aunt birthed me. From the medical standpoint, see, we had to be sure-enough emergency for Dr. Floyd. All the medicine for almost any type of pain, there was some type of herb in the woods. Even today, I still take hog huff tea for colds.

Emmett explained that the huff of a hog is the "toe" up and on the back of the hog's leg. "Take the huff off a hog. Then you parch it and make a tea." He went on to describe the central role that was played by the company's commissary.

It pretty well had everything the peoples in the quarters needed: your bacon, the rations, grits, meal come in big sacks. They had big wooden barrels they'd pour it in and dip it out whenever you went to buy it. There wasn't no money. The people that worked the turpentine once a month, when they paid you off, they'd deduct what you been charged. In a lot of instances, the people done used up what they made because there wasn't a whole lot of money. I can remember the best of bacon at that time was either three or five cents a pound. . . . I've forgotten what the wages was.

They had a truck, the same truck that hauled the turpentine out of the woods to the still, hauled food into the commissary. I don't know where their headquarters was. Every morning, the men gathered at the commissary and the still, getting ready to go to the woods to do their work. It'd be open then, and at midday. When the wood rider's out in the woods, it's closed. In the evening, it's open again. And every Saturday morning it was open.

The commissary also opened its doors to the white community, as Bea and Morley reported.

Morley: Anybody could buy.

Bea: Anybody could, because I went and got shoes out there. I think it was just mostly shoes and groceries.

Morley: They carried men's clothes. What they'd do, they would get something through the store. They hauled the spirits to Jacksonville with the truck, and while they were in Jacksonville, they'd load up feed for horses and mules, feed, groceries, store supplies, stuff like that. It was pretty good. Course the government did some help, too, in ways; surplus grain, they would distribute that. Now if I remember, might have been one or two years they gave grain out. I think they delivered that. I can't remember much about it, but I do remember some getting it.

There wasn't any money to give. Actually, the colored people out there, some of them, they traveled from one turpentine company to another. They come here, run up a big bill. They'd slip out at night and go to another place and get in there. That's the way they kept from paying the bills. And maybe the foremen out of this turpentine quarters would go to another and pick up a family. The man would come in and apply for a job—they needed labor—so they'd just slip in there at night and bring them on. They'd come in here and do the same thing.

JG: Wasn't this hard on the commissaries?

Morley: Well, they knew how to work that. They didn't pay them enough to start with. They didn't lose any money. If they'd lost money, they'd have been out of work, out of a job. Course they'd tell a lot of stories on those people, but they went to the doctor. Doctor charged five dollars. Manager of the turpentine would pay that and then charge the colored guy ten. See, that's what they tell. I don't know. That's just hearsay and gossip.

Jane W. Gibson

Few of the oldest graves in the black cemetery still have even unreadable markers such as this one (front left). The newer graves on the right belong to families who still bury their dead there, though they are from a town nearby.

NO VEGETABLES, NO TURPENTINE

Early fire stills, such as those found in and around Shellcracker Haven, were made like those used in Scotland to make whiskey. Hill (1950) writes that competition with other chemical industries spurred technological improvements in turpentine production. Beginning in the early 1900s, researchers working at the University of Florida Agricultural Experiment Stations, among other places, sought ways to promote conservation, production efficiency, and insurability of the naval stores industry—improvements that also restructured turpentine production. For example, steam distillation research, carried out in the 1940s, increased concentration of still ownership and turpentine production, with gum farming as a separate, subcontracted business. Before 1950, gum farmers and processors worked for the same company that owned and leased trees. In the new, "more efficient" industry, processors bought gum from farmers in a "continuous, labor-saving" system. By 1950, twenty-nine central steam stills produced 90% of the products. Only about 100 fire stills, such as those used in Shellcracker Haven, remained, down from 2,500 at their peak.

The federal government, through the Naval Stores Loan Program, stabilized and supported producer income and facilitated orderly distribution of gum naval stores. Loans were made available to members of the American Turpentine Farmers Association, members of the Agricultural Adjustment Administration's Naval Stores Conservation Program, and to others deemed by the United States Department of Agriculture (USDA) to follow good conservation practices. All had to sign a Producer's Marketing Agreement with the American Turpentine Farmers Association. Demand for turpentine in 1950 was high, and, with government support, prices were also high.

The decline of turpentining in the 1940s in Shellcracker Haven, then, had nothing to do with reduced demand, low prices, or with product substitution that came later on. According to Emmett, blacks began moving away from the quarters as opportunities for supplemental income declined. He explained that work for the still located near the larger town to the north could mean more ways "to do better," and when the still owner in Shellcracker Haven sold the land to a large, corporate pulpwood company, he did so in response to the loss of labor brought on by the decline in farming. For the buyer's part, the purchase made sense in light of growing demand for pulpwood products and timber.

By the early 1950s, Shellcracker Haven was all white except for the Bonners who owned their own farm. The still was sold in 1951, at the peak of the turpentine industry in Florida, but contracts that extended turpentine production from certain tracts were fulfilled, bringing the official end to the still quarters in the mid-1950s. I asked Morley and Bea about life after turpentine.

JG: Did the turpentiners move away?

Morley: Yeah.

JG: Could they have stayed to work on local farms?

Bea: There wasn't enough for them to live.

JG: When did turpentining stop?

Morley: That's going to be hard to say.

Bea: After you come back from the service.

Morley: What year would that be? I believe early '50s, because I went to work with [National Turpentine and Pulpwood] in December of '56. Within a year, they'd sold out to Illinois corporate [i.e., Owens-Illinois]. The turpentine was gone when they bought it.

JG: What happened to the quarters?

Bea: The houses were torn down.

JG: What did your dad do for work then?

Bea: He went to Jacksonville to work in the shipyard.

JG: Did the rest of you stay here and try to continue farming?

Bea: Yeah, because then, I think, my brothers farmed, about the same thing Daddy did: hogs and cows, vegetables.

JG: When did your mother quit farming?

Bea: She had to quit when the boys decided they wanted to do something else. She couldn't do it alone. As the kids got old enough, they got out and got jobs.

JG: Did they take care of her?

Bea: Yeah, and I think she was drawing a welfare check, and Daddy was sending them money.

JG: When were you in Apopka?

Morley: In the '50s, '52 to '56, somewhere in there. My work was commercial fishing, and I was here in Shellcracker Haven. And the fish were biting better; you could catch more fish down there. Couldn't catch them here like you could down in Lake and Orange County. My brother was down there, went down there and bought a new truck, boat, and motor. And I thought, I'm going to have something like that, too, but I didn't get them.

I'm not a fisherman. Well, I like it. It's just I didn't have the knack for knowing how to catch them. I'd fish right along with my oldest brother, and he'd catch twice as many as I did. I tried it for four years, and I made a living. I could make a little more fishing for myself than I could on public work, the type of work I could get to do because of the hourly wage or salary, but I finally had to give it up. It just wasn't enough. I'd go out today and maybe get 40 or 50 pounds, go tomorrow and maybe get two or three catfish. I couldn't make a living like that, so I quit, and I went out to public work. One reason, it was where I was. Well, then I could see where I could build a retirement, with a retirement program with the company. I was there twenty-five years and three months.

After the brief attempt at a career in fishing, Bea and Morley returned to Shellcracker Haven for good. Bea, along with at least one other wife of a frustrated fisherman, went to work in the county seat at a state-supported hospital for mentally and physically handicapped patients. The company that bought the turpentine still in 1951 and hired Morley in 1956 bought a great deal of the still-forested county that they converted to pine for timber and pulpwood.

JG: After twenty-five years, I hope you got more than a watch!

Morley: [shows me his wrist] That's the watch. It's been a good watch. Yeah, I worked there a long time.

JG: What did you do for the company?

Morley: Everything they did, but sit in the office: site preparation, surveying other people's property, making pine ceilings, tractor operating, bulldozing work, everything. When Owens-Illinois bought them out, they kept the same workmen and crew. Wasn't any change of personnel.

Bea: [And] a little bit of farming, but not too much.

The related story of the decline of small farming in Shellcracker Haven shows the reciprocal relationship between turpentine production and farming. As farms began to go out of business, black families lost their supplemental income; as they moved from the still quarters to the town up the highway, remaining farmers lost their primary source of labor. Beyond the boundaries of the community, restructuring of the naval stores industry and U.S. agriculture set the stage for Morley and others to change careers, and for commercial fishing to dominate Shellcracker Haven's economy.

REMEMBERING THE LAKE

At night, when the air cooled and years of experience taught that fishing would improve, fishermen tied one end of a great net to a tree or to another fishing boat and stretched the seine into a semicircle back to the lake shore. There men hauled in the net and unloaded its "pocket" for processing.

Commercial freshwater fishing may never have been especially important to the state of Florida, but it was always significant in Shellcracker Haven. It began in the 19th century on Shellcracker Lake, though no one who lives in the town today knows who the first commercial fishermen were. Mrs. Jameson, whose family came to the area under the Armed Occupation Act of 1842, claims that none of her ancestors fished for a living. In fact, with scorn for that way of life, she assured me, "I never ate cooter" (a kind of turtle). Morley's grandfather may well have been among the first to make a living from the lake, but he did so as a seasonal supplement to farm-ing, as many farmers undoubtedly did. The Knight family, descended from a William Knight shown on the 1880 census, may have been the first full-time commercial fish-ermen in Shellcracker Haven.

A local old-timer told the writer of a Florida sporting magazine that, as a child, he watched the backbreaking labor required to pull in, hand over hand, a huge net. Its size required the use of a 30-foot wooden boat, much bigger than the streamlined, fiberglass versions seen on Florida lakes today. Another story appeared in a local newspaper in 1918. Two commercial netters used a 700-yard seine to make a day-time catch so big that it took three hours for three people to remove the fish from the net, and it took three boat trips to get the fish to the packinghouse, remembered locally as the "fish house." Catfish made up over 6,000 of the more than 7,000 pounds of marketable fish, and the skinning crew worked steadily from Wednesday afternoon until noon on Thursday to dress and prepare the catch for market.

The fish in Shellcracker Lake took on importance in many ways for the people of the town. Through successful fishing, men earned status; sale of fish and fishing equipment and services brought cash rewards; production and processing integrated families; barter and sale integrated the community; and fishing gave the town the identity it carries today.

The elders I spoke to about commercial fishing remembered the fish house as a simple wooden structure that sat at the end of a pier as early as 1905. The daughter of a fisherman believes it was built long before then out of cypress grown and milled on the lake. From here, catfish went to Kansas City, Missouri, and Jacksonville; scale fish, also called **panfish,** went to southern Georgia and other parts of Florida.

Two unrelated families in the town each claimed the fish house as their own. The question became of vital importance to the community when a new family purchased the right-of-way from the railroad and tried to close the pier. The Knight family, among others, had long tied their boats there, and they still needed access to the fish house. The Knights filed suit to settle matters, and subpoenaed Mr. Peck to testify on their behalf. Mr. Peck's daughter, Beth, remembered vividly the day that turned into tragedy for her family:

> The community back then, as it does today, had a reputation for some pretty rough goings-on around, and there was a lot of nights I can remember as a child waking up with some-body beating on our back door, saying, "Mr. Peck, Mr. Peck! I'm in trouble." And it would be someone with a law officer that needed bail to get out or something. Usually it had to do with drinking, and they'd get into a fight with some of the local men. It wasn't any-thing vicious.
>
> Right in front of my parents' store there was a fish house, and this is where the men brought their fish to clean them; and, well, at that time, they didn't clean them so much as they did pack them in ice for shipping. But they were allowed to sell scale fish as well as catfish at that time, and they would come in and pack up their fish down there in ice. And there was a little railroad car, a little flatcar that I rode many times up and down that little hill, that went up to the sidetrack, the second track of the Seaboard. And they would ship these fish in barrels. They would set off cars, boxcars, there, and they would ship these in barrels.
>
> This boat landing down there had this old building on it. I was allowed to go down, as long as the fishermen were not working down there, and fish because it was right directly in front of my parents' place, and they could see what I was doing. Saturday night and

Sunday, the fish house was off-limits to any of the children because this was where the men gathered up. They had their drinks and their poker parties, and sometimes they had some rough times down there, but they usually kept it down there. But sometimes on Saturday night was when my Daddy would get the knock.

When did Daddy die? Anyway, some years ago, when this property began to sell along [the lake edge], and the old depot burned, a family purchased this property where this boat dock had been. The people who purchased it had planned to extend their property, which was included in this purchase, to close this landing, and they carried this to court; and my father was asked to come in and testify as to how long this had been, in his knowledge, a public landing. And he did, not feeling well, and my mother was sitting in the car across the street waiting to drive him home. And he asked to be called first because he wasn't feeling well, and he passed away sitting in the witness chair for this property.

The dispute with the landing was resolved in favor of it keeping open as a public land-ing, and today is where the boat ramp is for the county. The fishermen no longer keep their boats there. They did for awhile before it was made into a county park, but, as I said before, most of them, or all of them, have their own boats, motors, trailers, and trucks, and they don't fish in Shellcracker Lake as much as they did.

As Beth hinted, the fish house was an important social center for Shellcracker Haven. I heard stories about rowdy Saturday night poker games going on inside where some drank "the lightning" that moonshiners from across the lake traded for fish. "Ladies," like children, never went in on Saturday nights when sometimes the gambling and drinking led to fist- or gunfights over women, money, or old insults. These quarrels seldom ended in serious physical harm to anyone, but the threat of violence was usually enough to keep some at bay and others in line. Outside Shellcracker Haven, the town's reputation as a wild and dangerous place grew with every conflagration, and today this reputation continues to ward off most outsiders.

During the day, children played around the fish house, languishing in small, wooden boats or hanging bamboo poles from the dock into the tea-colored water. Tannins, a natural product of cypress and other highly acidic litter that fall into and break down in the water, give the lake its color. Here is Beth's description of that time:

> I used to sit on the end of the dock and fish, mostly little turtles that took your bait. And I learned early to bait a hook and take turtles and whatever else bit my hook off, because my mother would carry me fishing, but she said, "If you're going to fish, you're going to have to do everything for yourself."
>
> The fishing was great. It was prior to any restriction on what you could catch or when you could catch it, and we had fish that you would not believe. You could go out most any time in season and catch all the bream that you wanted, or speckled perch. My friend Suzanne, she and I spent many hours when we were young teenagers on the lake. We fished and we caught fish. We cooked fish, and even after we got old enough to have boyfriends, we did the same thing. We just really kind of lived on the lake.

As Emmett's story suggested, the fish from Shellcracker Lake took on new importance during the Depression. Cash became scarce, and fish substituted in local barter arrangements as coin for other kinds of food, tools, and anything available in the commissary. Farmers traded vegetables, chickens, and other animal products for fish, and families from the still quarters traded greens grown in small gardens. Fish integrated the community, and it was more important than money when, as Sarah put it, "Money didn't do you no good because there wasn't nothing to buy." Sarah, who came to Shellcracker Haven as a young mother with her husband, remembered the role she played in making fish available to families in the still quarters:

> He wasn't a very big boy. His daddy was in the crowd. He worked there, too. But this lit-tle colored, little black boy come up here one evening. Also we had a big fish box in back. We bought fish and sold them.
>
> This little black boy come up to me one evening and said, "Mrs. S., do you have a fish I could buy for fifteen cents?" and I said, "Yes." I didn't have. I said, "Yes, I know I could find you one." He went on running round the house, and I opened the fish box and reached in there and got him two. I didn't even put them on the scales. And he handed me the fif-teen cents, and I give him the two fish. He said, "This will make all I can eat, Mrs. S. When I go home I'm going to cook them and sit down, eat every one of them. Eat every bit of it."
>
> I didn't know but what maybe I might have started something with him, but you know, he never did come back and ask me for more fish without money to pay for them.

The Depression worked little hardship on most families of Shellcracker Haven because of the town's food self-sufficiency, and because few who lived there had ever enjoyed the higher standard of living experienced by people in cities with elec-tricity and indoor plumbing. Meat became scarce, as did shortening and a few other items such as automobile tires, but increased availability of these through a "black market" in the county seat could supply those willing to make the trip and able to pay the higher prices. All asserted they had most of what they needed because they pro-duced it themselves or could trade what they produced with someone who had what they wanted. Kin and friendship ties, including Mr. Peck's store, assured everyone a share. In Sarah's words:

> Peck's store ran accounts for practically everyone in the community, you know—a week or two weeks. And I fared a little better than some of them did because Mrs. Peck and myself was real good friends. All of us was back then. And if she got anything in the store, I'd be sure to get my part of it. So we did about as fair as some did.
>
> I traded some in [another town,] and they had some meat and I wanted me some. And she said I didn't trade there often enough to get it. She wouldn't let me have none. And I said, "Well, you know one thing. I could get it in [the county seat]. I could go right out there and get in my car and go and get me some meat." She said, "Well, that's the black market." I said, "I don't care how black the market is if my children ain't got their piece of meat." So I went and got it.

Sarah and her husband, like Morley's father, bought fish to retail from other fish-ing families in the town, and so did not make regular use of the fish house or of the pier. We sat outside on Sarah's front porch, facing the lake across the town's one paved road. She pointed to a site about a hundred yards north of where the public landing stands today, and there identified her family's lake entrance where she rented boats built by her husband. As she described it:

> I fished when I wanted to. When I wanted to go fishing, I went down there and got in the boat and picked up a paddle and went on. I tended his fishing company to the fishing part of it. There was a dock down in there where we had our boats, and I've been down there many a morning before daylight. It were freezing putting out boats. They were scared they wouldn't get a boat. They'd come sit out there in the bonnets and wait for it to get light enough where they could fish.

Jane W. Gibson

"Money didn't do you no good because there wasn't nothing to buy."

Now understand, I didn't fish, and I didn't dress no fish. After my husband quit selling down there, we had a box here of our own, and I weighed the fish in and I weighed them out.

The Pecks lived well from the income generated by fishing and farming in Shellcracker Haven. Before the town received electricity, while everyone else depended on kerosene lamps for light and wood for heating, this family owned its own generator and purchased new cars for which they paid cash. Yet, in this close-knit, kin-based community, the Peck's good fortune was everyone's good fortune. Mr. Peck gave rides to other towns, and as late as 1990, his son-in-law still "ran tabs," interest-free, for some who could not pay. The Peck's store remained in the family for nearly seventy years, until late 1991 when the rising costs of buying and keeping small quantities on the shelves exceeded its income.

When the Depression ended, the families of Shellcracker Haven say they hardly knew it had come and gone. Mr. Knight became a WWII veteran and returned to Shellcracker Haven to take up where he'd left off. But then life took a turn for the worse. Mr. Peck's testimony that helped save the fish house did not save commercial freshwater fishing. The families of Shellcracker Haven, having adjusted after the economic restructuring of agriculture and the naval stores industries, entered what the owner of Blue's Garage called "the starvin' time," when the state put a stop to seining. Legal commercial fishing now meant catfishing with trotlines, a method that substantially reduced fishermen's abilities to support their families. Some, including Mr. Knight, took up nighttime seining. Under cover of darkness, and some say in boats painted black, they navigated "behind the hill" and continued to fish. The Florida Game and Fresh Water Fish Commission (GFC) was serious about its new authority, however, and enforcement meant expropriation of boats and all associated equipment as well. With improved surveillance and increased numbers of field personnel, the costs of illegal seining soon exceeded the benefits, and even Mr. Knight, known affectionately to the GFC as "a great pirate," had to give it up. Nor did the fish house survive after the county's condemnation proceedings; someone burned the building to the ground.

A few women—those with cars or with friends who had cars—took on wage labor jobs in larger towns nearby. Government subsidies became essential to household survival. Although food stamps and other government assistance were not new in Shellcracker Haven (Bea's mother received government aid, as did some elderly Knights), the period following the end of seining and the outlawing of panfish sales increased the need for outside help. Government assistance became a part of the community economy that, of necessity, diversified to take advantage of the growing interest in recreational fishing. An unpublished report in 1958 showed five fish camps, none locally owned, with a total of twenty cabins and ninety-eight boats for rent along the town's lake edge.

Towns to the north and south maintained hotel facilities, and advertising promoted the recreational hunting and fishing opportunities of the area. With the growth of the tourist industry, some in Shellcracker Haven took advantage of the demand for fish guides, bait, and boats, and the Peck's store began to prosper with increased patronage.

Commercial fishermen did not fare so well. A launch carried fishers out into Shellcracker Lake to put out their trotlines for awhile, but families struggled to make the transition to the reduced catch. Some remember a crash of the catfish population in Shellcracker Lake that, they say, drove them to fish other lakes of the region. That meant buying trucks and trailers as well as gasoline. A fish company delivered a freezer to Mr. Knight's shed, and the company's refrigerated truck replaced the train that, by the time the dying still quarters twitched for the last time, no longer stopped in the community.

Some people harvested oranges and vegetables from the muck farm nearby. One young man caught stray cats for a researcher, and his mother anesthetized frogs. Mr. Knight gathered moss and tried working for the American Can Company, which kept moving him around the state but never to a location near his home. Morley gave up fishing and farming altogether and went to work for Owens-Illinois. Everyone had to "hustle" to make ends meet, but this was something the townspeople's history of adjustments to forces beyond their control had taught them how to do.

The early history of Shellcracker Haven shows how thoroughly integrated families' social and working lives were, and how the community's internal cohesion— that sense of obligation beyond one's own gate—contributed to every family's survival. Even the historical racism that segregated the still quarters could not prevent the penetration of that formidable boundary when families could meet each other's needs by crossing it. Ancestors of today's families in Shellcracker Haven were among the pioneer settlers whose courage and adventurous spirit would be celebrated in history. They made their living with their own hands applied directly to the land, the forests, and the lakes of the region. To this living they felt entitled, because they worked for the fruits of nature's bounty provided by God. The state's active involvement in the management of freshwater fish and wildlife, the subject of the next chapter, changed this relationship and changed the community.

3/Fishermen to Pirates;
Fish Bailiffs to Biologists

This chapter tells the story of how state management of Florida's fisheries and wildlife came about. It tells how small-scale commercial fishermen lost control over the fisheries on which they and their families depended. And it tells how today's Florida Fish and Wildlife Conservation Commission (FWC) grew out of the Florida Game and Fresh Water Fish Commission (GFC), which grew out of many earlier agency incarnations. The social and political history of today's FWC helps us understand something of an "agency personality" that describes people who are proud of the professional work they do; self-assured because they believe in the power of science and the rightness of their cause; and dedicated to carrying out the FWC's conservation mission while protecting the agency through political savvy and carefully managed public relations.

To avoid confusion, when I refer to the GFC, I am referring to the agency in its longest and most significant developmental phase that endured for over a half-century, from the mid-1940s until the late 1990s. When I use the acronym FWC, I refer to the agency as it is structured and named today. The acronyms GFC and FWC should be understood as abbreviations representing, respectively, earlier and more recent names for what is essentially the same agency: Personnel, infrastructure, mission, and method remain about the same.

The FWC oversees marine fisheries, which is a significant expansion of the agency's authority. Some minor restructuring occurred as well, though that will not affect our understanding of the issues at hand: the consequences for Shellcracker Haven and similar communities, the health and longevity of Florida's **biodiversity,** and the relationship between natural resource-dependent communities and biodiversity. We'll see in this chapter how state fish and wildlife management evolved from its early clumsy and halting steps to become the powerful, sophisticated organization that it is. The FWC is an autonomous agency whose decisions cannot be appealed nor second-guessed or contradicted by the state legislature. It is sensitive to public perceptions and invests significantly in public relations and education. It is committed to its conservation mission pursued through good science and law, enforced by its own well-equipped, well-trained wildlife police force.

EARLY STAKEHOLDERS

The first commercial fishers of Shellcracker Haven sold more than catfish from their nets. They sold the occasional alligator hide and panfish. These included bass, shellcrackers, and bream (a collective term for several varieties of sunfish), though the proportion of these fish to catfish was small. Local fishermen also used their nets to eliminate "trash fish," also called **rough fish,** from the lake. Fishermen believed, and fisheries biologists confirmed, that gar, mudfish, and shad competed with marketable species. Seining, fishermen claimed, helped clear the lake bottom of the unwanted vegetation that has since overtaken the lake more than once, and whose control now is undertaken with aquatic herbicides.

Commercial fishing on a large scale had been practiced in Florida's freshwaters since before 1890 (DeQuine 1948:39). Early on, the GFC recognized two main freshwater systems as having commercial significance: the St. Johns River and Lake Okeechobee. Of the communities located adjacent to these waters, the GFC estimated that 2,500 persons were directly or indirectly dependent upon the fishing industry. In 1945, their total catch was estimated at roughly 1.5 million pounds of bream, 850,000 pounds of crappie, and 4.8 million pounds of catfish and bullheads valued at over $1.54 million. Other commercially utilized lakes came to the attention of the GFC—Lakes George, Harris, Crescent, and Reedy—but no research on the impact of commercial fishing on the lakes of Shellcracker Basin was ever conducted "due to limitations of trained personnel, and to avoid the danger of over-extending the activities" (DeQuine, 1952:26).

The most common methods of taking commercial species were haul seines such as those used on Shellcracker Lake, wire pots and traps that Shellcracker fishermen located in the **bonnets** (water lilies), trotlines, pound nets, and hoop nets. Eddie Knight's father, like many of the people of Shellcracker Haven, depended on commercial fishing for the majority of his income. He seined and bought fish from others to retail, and Eddie remembers "twenty-five or thirty" people catching fish all the time in the late 1940s and early 1950s. If each of these represented a single household, it would be safe to say that fully half of Shellcracker Haven engaged in commercial fishing. This number does not include those who, like Morley, thought of themselves as farmers who fished in the off-season.

Another industry grew alongside commercial fishing in Florida's lakes, and it would ultimately eliminate the use of seines on which Shellcracker Haven's fishing families depended. This business relied on tourists, the recreational fishers and hunters who bought licenses from the management agency and came with money to lake towns where they rented boats and cabins; bought food, bait, and fishing and hunting equipment; and hired guides to show them the best locations in which to enjoy their sport.

Florida's tourist industry began its recognizable growth after the Civil War. William D. Kelly described in 1885 how Floridians made a living: "We live on sweet potatoes and consumptive Yankees" and "We sell atmosphere" (Kelly 1888). Already just six miles north of Shellcracker Haven but still well within the lake region, W. S. Moore opened a hotel that catered to hunters and fishers from all over the country. The menu offered "quail with every meal when in season," and the Chamber of Commerce of that town claimed the hotel served over 2,500 game birds in a single season.

Jane W. Gibson

Shellcracker fishermen set wire pots and traps in the bonnets (water lilies) to catch commercial species.

Rapid growth in Florida's tourist industry, and the most significant for Shellcracker Haven, occurred toward the end of World War II. Much of the state's tourist industry was transformed by the needs of wartime to accommodate the military. By 1945, Shellcracker Haven hosted three fish camps, all within the space of a quarter mile, and the town gained a reputation as a booming fishing community. Across the railroad tracks that ran parallel to the water's edge, but still a stone's throw from the lake, Jake Williams, an English immigrant, placed a barracks building purchased from Camp Blanding. He then converted it to three separate cabins and rented them between 1947 and 1959 to recreational fishers, from Georgia and Florida mostly, but also from Alabama, Ohio, Virginia, Tennessee, North Carolina, and Pennsylvania. By the time tourists checked in to Williams's cabins, the nature of commercial fishing in Florida had changed completely.

THE RISE OF A CONSERVATION AGENCY AND ITS CULTURE

Today, the FWC manages Florida's fish and game. The Commission might best be seen as the latest of many legislative attempts at fair and effective conservatorship in a turbulent political environment. It has survived budgetary challenges, contestation between managers and legislators and between the state and its counties, and at least one big battle: the one that transformed the agency when commercial freshwater fisher families lost their main source of income.

The Fish Bailiff and the Posse

Before the first settlers arrived in Shellcracker Haven around 1846, the game and fish had already become the property of the territory. Yet, without rules to enforce, the sovereign could not act on its legal authority. So, the territorial government and counties—with no coordination among rule-makers and in piecemeal, reactive fashion—passed lots of rules. In 1828, the territorial legislature prohibited fire hunting west of the Suwannee River and, after eleven months, extended the prohibition to the east, realizing perhaps that their rationale would be valid on both sides of the river. In 1832, they disallowed the damming of navigable streams for over 24 hours if fish were prevented from passing upstream. In 1851, Escambia and Santa Rosa counties began to regulate hunting. In 1877, in response to an urban fashion demand for the flamboyant feathers of Florida's giant egrets, flamingos, and other well-dressed birds, the state legislature passed protection statutes for plumage birds, their nests, eggs, and their young. They also protected shad in spawning season in 1893 and, first among the states to enact such a law, fixed a **bag limit** for turkeys in 1895.

Now with rules on the books, the legislature recognized the need for field personnel to enforce them. In 1881, the sheriff of each county became a special agent of the state known as a "fish bailiff." The fish bailiff could appoint as many deputies as he needed and "summon a sufficient posse" to enforce the provisions of the law relating to fish. The bailiff and his posse, upon capture of a suspected offender, could make an arrest and carry the party before a magistrate for trial. As part of the sentence, the magistrate could confiscate any of the offender's tools, including boats, nets, tackle, and anything else used in violation of the law, a provision that continues to act as a deterrent today. The magistrate could then sell confiscated properties at an auction to the highest bidder.

Game Wardens, a Department, and a Commission

After 1899, a county with fifty registered voters and taxpayers could petition the state for a **game warden** whose responsibilities expanded those of the fish bailiff to include enforcement of game laws. With the recommendation of the county commissioners, the governor would appoint a county resident to fill the position for a two-year term—or, in the absence of a game warden, the county sheriff enforced the laws concerning fish and wild game.

By the time the Knight family arrived late in the 19th century, their county had one game warden, but the warden's ability to enforce the rules for the entire area was limited. In 1913, the legislature created the first Department of Game and Fish as well as the office of State Game and Fish Commissioner. Things changed in 1915 when ownership and title to all wild birds and game were vested in the counties of Florida and the legislature replaced the Department with the Shell Fish Commission.

The establishment of the first Department of Game and Fish is not without interest, however, even though it lasted such a short time. As part of the act that created it, the Commissioner became accountable to the legislature for reporting all revenues from licenses and penalties, and had to see to publication of all laws relating to fish and game. By 1925, there were some 175 local laws on the books, many of which conflicted. Differences between counties created difficulties for legislators who owed their jobs to tiny local constituencies. A number of court cases further complicated matters by challenging the constitutionality of vesting management of fish and wild game in the state. Though the courts consistently upheld the state's authority, state legislators sought ways to unburden themselves of the political turmoil surrounding game and fish management.

Another Department, a New Commissioner, and Another Commission

With county-level management in place, the state legislature created the Department of Game and Fresh Water Fish in 1927. To head this organization, the governor appointed "one competent person" to fill the position of State Game Commissioner for a four-year term. The duties of the Commissioner were defined as enforcement of all laws of the State of Florida relating to game, nongame birds, freshwater fish, and fur-bearing animals, for which he was to receive an annual salary of $6,000 (about $58,000 in 2003 dollars) plus travel and expenses. To secure his appointment, the Commissioner had to give bond in a sum of $10,000 (about $100,000 in 2003), and his assistants paid bonds of a minimum $1,000 (about $10,000 in 2003).

In support of the State Game Commissioner, and showing awareness of the rapid rate at which developers were transforming wild Florida into urban landscapes, the legislature created a Wild Life Conservation Commission. This board was to be made up of Florida residents with intimate knowledge of fish and game. Their duties were to assist and advise the State Game Commissioner in the establishment of fish hatcheries, game farms and game and fresh-water fish breeding grounds and state game refuges, and in the acquisition of State game lands. The potential financial contributions of recreational hunting and fishing had clearly spurred expansion of the state's interest in managing wildlife.

New responsibilities required people and infrastructure. The Department of Game and Fresh Water Fish rounded out its bureaucratic milieu with new buildings, offices, clerical help, office supplies, and other equipment. These expenses, like all others, were paid from the state game fund, along with the costs of "printing and publishing bulletins and other publications" and the costs of publishing other media to disseminate information from the game commissioner's office. Money, then and now, is a singularly important limiting factor for growth and development of fish and wildlife management. The first monies came from county judges who collected fines and various kinds of license fees for hunting and fishing.

In spite of a 1929 law that returned "ownership" of wildlife to the state, the legislature left open at least one loophole. They passed laws to try to coordinate game and freshwater fish management, but county governments continued to exercise their own regulatory authority, sometimes in conflict with state authority, permitted them under the same article. In fact, some county governments even created their own game commissions (GFC 1968).

More Commissions and a Board

In 1933, the legislature substituted the State Conservation Commission for the Department of Game and Fresh Water Fish. The new Commission was composed of the Governor of Florida, the Secretary of State, the Attorney General, the

Comptroller, the State Treasurer, the State Superintendent of Public Instruction, and the Commissioner of Agriculture. All properties, accounts, obligations, moneys, duties, and powers formerly vested in the State Geologist, the Shellfish Commissioner, and the State Game Commissioner, all of whose offices and departments were abolished, now came under a Board of Conservation. This effort at streamlining game and fish management went the way of all others, and in 1935, the state legislature created a Commission of Game and Fresh Water Fish. After another six years and passage of more than 150 new local laws, the legislature passed, with the necessary three-fifths majority in both the House and the Senate, an amendment to the Florida Constitution that established the Florida Game and Fresh Water Fish Commission, the GFC, in 1942. Constitutional status protected the agency from legislative caprice in establishing and dismantling management agencies and in manipulating management itself with control over the agency's budget. In a public referendum on the matter, the electorate concurred and the new commission endured until 1998.

> From and after January 1, 1943, the management, restoration, conservation, and regulation, of the birds, game, fur bearing animals, and fresh water fish, of the State of Florida, and the acquisition, establishment, control, and management, of hatcheries, sanctuaries, refuges, reservations, and all other property now or hereafter owned or used for such purposes by the State of Florida, shall be vested in a Commission to be known as the Game and Fresh Water Fish Commission. (Constitution of the State of Florida, 1885, Article IV, Section 30)

A FAUSTIAN BARGAIN

In 1946, the GFC took the first steps in its new and powerful capacity as a constitutional agency to eliminate the commercial freshwater fishing industry. These measures were taken in fulfillment of an agreement with sports fishers who agreed to support the constitutional amendment that would create the agency and give it autonomy. In exchange, the agency prohibited the use of most commercial fishing technologies in public waters, prohibited the sale of game fish (black bass, crappie, redbreast, bluegill, shellcrackers, bream, pickerel, and pike), and limited the legal gear by which catfish and rough fish might be taken. These actions resulted directly from political pressure exerted by organized sport fishers who believed that commercial fishing undermined sport fishing. With the stroke of a pen in the state capitol, Florida's traditional commercial freshwater fishermen were transformed into outlaws.

How the GFC participated in this contentious debate reveals much about the politics of natural resource management in the state. And it is ultimately politics that has undermined the agency's mission. For all their legal authority, sophisticated research, and enforcement technologies, the agency remains virtually powerless to stem the tide of development and urban expansion that continues to cause species declines in Florida.

I visited John Dequine, his real name, in his Florida home where he permitted me to tape our conversation. "Jack" was the first fisheries biologist hired by the GFC in its new constitutional status; and along with the fishing families themselves, he was among the first casualties in the battle over commercial freshwater fishing. Though he no longer worked for the state when I met him, he continued fisheries research and consulting on fisheries restocking and management. The desk in the small office was covered with papers and journals and all the trappings of a researcher's work. Here is his story, which does not appear as part of the "official" history of the agency even though it was a GFC fisheries biologist who suggested I meet him.

Jack: I started working for the Florida Game and Freshwater Fish Commission in October 1946. I was employed by the then director Dr. Kennedy in response to this controversy that had arisen between the people who identified themselves as sport fishermen or recreational fishermen and the commercial fishermen who had been operating in the large lakes of Florida since it was settled. And the area you're interested in, they were part of this whole commercial fisheries industry and was operated by people who had been there, I guess, for generations. At least that's the way I found it when I arrived in '46.

Of course, it was a big political hassle. That was all the fighting, in the '46 session I think it was, of the legislature and the following '48 session. It was over this: whether or not they were going to allow this commercial fishing and how much of it they were going to allow. I was supposed to come in and find the answer to the problem: Can there be commercial fishing or should there be commercial fishing? Let me put it [another way]. The question was: Is commercial fishing damaging to recreational fishing? Are the commercial fishermen raping the waters, ruining the habitat for game fish?

There are a lot of things involved in here, economics of course. The economics of Florida residents who made their living in commercial fishing as well as the economics of Florida residents who, by this time, were catering to the bass fishermen and sports fishermen. And this was, I would say, the essence of the battle. Those on the sport fishing side claimed that the commercial fishermen were ruining sport fishing and they couldn't go out and catch them like they did in the years before. You still hear that today, that they can't catch them like they did ten years ago. Well this was in '46 and they couldn't catch them like they could in '36 and if you'd been here in '36, I'm sure they would have said the same thing about '26. That was the crux of it. There were more recreational fishermen every year gaining by leaps and bounds.

JG: Why did the GFC prioritize recreational fishing?

Jack: The reason was that in 1943, through the efforts of the Florida Wildlife Federation and other sportsmen's groups, [the legislature passed] a constitutional amendment that created the GFC. Well, the reason that the sportsmen's groups did that was that there had been such a hodgepodge of local fishing and hunting laws scattered all over the state, county to county. The laws would change, and the sportsmen of Florida felt that it needed to be standardized and unified for the whole state. Furthermore, there was little effectiveness to the law enforcement; the sportsmen felt the law enforcement needed to be more effective.

Many of the old-time game wardens were appointed because they helped that particular state senator get elected. That's the old way, a political patronage system. That's the way the game warden, matter of fact, all of the employees were appointed, through the political patronage system. No merit. No experience. No training or anything else. Matter of fact, the first professionally trained people in that were Earl Frye, who later became director, and I, and we were both hired in '46. He was in charge of game and I was in charge of fish. And that was kind of a process of evolution from the old political patronage system of administering the laws of the fish and game to a system which hopefully relied on fact-finding, and at least the scientific approach and managing of the resources supposedly for the betterment of all people.

Now, they gave it the power to make the rules and regulations, and it also gave them the power to enforce them. The only thing it did not give them the power to do was appropriate the money which the legislature retained for its own purposes, which it still does today. The legislature is the one that sets the costs of licenses or whatever other fees the game commission receives. The only restriction on that is that, in order to qualify for federal aid in fish and wildlife restoration, all of those licenses and fees must be earmarked for use by game and fish administration. It can't be diverted to schools or roads or anything else.

It took most of the politics and political patronage away from the legislators and placed it in the hands of a five-man commission whose terms would be staggered with the hope and desire that that would eliminate, for example, complete wipeouts of the personnel every time there was a change of administration. And it pretty well did that.

JG: It seems strange to me that the legislature would voluntarily give up its authority.

Jack: It was unusual, but there was an awful lot of pressure from the recreational fishermen and hunters that got the legislature to put it on the ballot. And then it was accepted by a pretty large landslide, and it's been tested two or three times since then. And the people of Florida are not willing to go back to the old system. They have affirmed their desire to have that type of commission where it was separated from the political administration.

JG: Were the recreational fishers well organized?

Jack: Pretty well. They put on a lot of pressure. Florida Wildlife Federation, that was the key or probably the main collection group of all the interests that were pushing this thing because they realized they had to have a kind of united front.

JG: What was the relationship like between the GFC and the legislature after the amendment passed?

Jack: A lot of legislators didn't like it, of course. The ones from the commercial fishing counties didn't like it. Well, the political power of the commercial fishing legislators was sufficient to declare Okeechobee a saltwater lake, for purposes of administration.

JG: When the GFC became a constitutional agency, what other changes came about as a result?

Jack: A lot of expansion took place, but they also went out of state and got an experienced director by name of Ben Morgan who had been director in the state of Alabama for a number of years. He came in and, among a number of other things, they started schools for their enforcement people and they put them in uniforms and they hired more of them. Now that they had earmarked funds and a buildup for a couple of years since the initiation of the constitutional amendment, they had more funds to work with. And so they progressed in this manner. Then they immediately started employing more biologists, both fish and game.

They relied on what the legislature appropriated each year, but that could change. If the preponderance of the legislature got mad at what the game department did, they could cut them way down. Hard to run a program that way. I have an empathy with those administrators back in those days. They had to constantly be politicking to pay the salaries of their people.

JG: On what did the Commission base its decision to eliminate certain commercial fishing technologies? The economics of the importance of the tourist industry in Florida versus the economics of commercial fishing?

Jack: These were considerations that they took into account in their deliberations. There was legislative pressure both ways, depending on which legislator you talked to. All over

Florida there were like city or county fish and game clubs, and they all contributed to the Florida Wildlife Federation, which became the one organization which represented all of the recreational fishermen and hunters in the state.

JG: What were the arguments against the technologies?

Jack: The reason for doing that was simply the vocal and printed pressure, the media pressure from these groups of recreational people scattered all over the state. It was their claims that commercial fishing was destroying the bass beds, was eliminating the bass, taking the bluegill and shellcracker and crappie by the tons to northern markets. It was their claim that some of this was going on, but the extent of it was not known and what impact it had on the water in which it was occurring was not known.

They kept arguing back and forth. They had the University of Miami make a brief study to try to answer this question: Is commercial fishing hurting sport fishing? Their conclusion was that there was no evidence to indicate that commercial fishing was damaging sport fishing, and that's about the time that, among other things, created a kind of steamroller effect. And that's why they finally decided to hire a fisheries biologist to try to find these answers.

JG: But that was after the rule had already been passed to eliminate seining.

Jack: Oh yeah. The rules had already been passed, but the decision to do some fact-finding studies was just based on the continued controversy. The only data they had was admittedly lacking. They had a system of collecting records on how many fish were shipped out of the state and so on and so forth, but it was based purely on voluntary submission by the fish dealers. And the only thing we could do to use as a basis was to get those records and assume that the degree and inclination of error in them remained the same year after year. Because there was no indication in those records that the commercial fishermen were overharvesting the crop that was being produced.

JG: You mentioned in one of your articles that it was assumed they would underreport for tax purposes.

Jack: I may have said that. Yeah, I did feel that they probably underreported. Wholesale fish dealers. You see, the arrangement of this commercial fishing industry, the fish dealer is the main man. He provided the money, the nets, the equipment, and then did the marketing for these fishing crews. This was on Okeechobee or on Lake George. There were also some who were able to do it independently. Most of them, let's say, were financed by the fish dealers.

JG: Where did the fish dealers come from? Were they former fishermen themselves?

Jack: Most of them got a little ahead and got more into the marketing than into the actual harvesting and got other people to do the harvesting. The other people didn't have the finances to buy the nets and boats and equipment it took, so this is pretty standard all up and down the east coast.

A typical fishing crew would have had two powerboats. It would have had a mile of net, a mile-long seine. It would have had two or three other boats and about five men altogether, a typical fishing crew. And there were, I think—this was on Okeechobee—I think there were nine or ten crews operating, and about the same thing up on Lake George.

The crews [in Shellcracker Basin] were, I would say, probably not as large, or their operations were not as large. They were not working in as large a body of water, and it seems to me, as I recall, there were several different family groups or independent groups without the leadership of a large fish dealer that you found in the other areas.

JG: They used smaller nets?

Jack: Nine hundred yards, that would be a big net for those lakes, but as I recall, most of them were about three or four hundred yards, which three men can operate, and they wouldn't have needed a large powerboat to drag the nets that the big fishermen needed.

JG: Were the commercial fishermen organized?

Jack: There was no single organization that spoke for the commercial fishermen. Butler Dowda [member of the House of Representatives] from Putnam County spoke for commercial fishermen from Lake George. Bill Hendry from Okeechobee County spoke for the fishermen down there, and a fellow named Pierce. He was the state senator from down there. These people were usually the spokesmen for the commercial fishermen. They would attend the meetings, or sometimes a fish dealer [would attend]. Bill Hendry happened to be a fish dealer, too. Everything was volunteer back then. There were no paid lobbyists. I'd say the nearest thing approaching that would have been the president of the Florida Wildlife Federation, whoever he happened to be at that time.

The governors tried to ride the fence. You could say that the only one that I saw was really, you might say, was biased, or leaned definitely one way or another, was McCarty. His actions were done at the demand of people. It became an issue in the '48 campaign, and McCarty was all for the sportsmen, and the Wildlife Federation ganged up on McCarty's side.

JG: Was your research supported by the GFC and the staff?

Jack: For the most part, my research was supported. There were a few dissenters. Not that they dissented with the scientific findings. They dissented on the timing of our recommendations and the extent of our recommendations. When McCarty came in, he appointed two commissioners who, at the behest of the Florida Wildlife people, were definitely anticommercial fishermen, and they made no bones about it, and so that had an influence.

JG: Today the Chamber of Commerce is vocal on this issue. Did they play a role then?

Jack: Yeah. We had them both ways. We had the outdoor press both ways. Some supported our position that a limited amount of commercial fishing could take place without damage to sport fishermen; others claimed it was all bad. The Chamber of Commerce, their argument—it's a good argument, but I'm not convinced the data are there to back it up—is that recreational fishing provides more monetary return to the state of Florida than does commercial fishing, and there is some evidence for that, but the point is: Is the activity of commercial fishing having any major impact on that income that's coming from recreational fishing? That's always been the question. Or at least that's the question in rational people's minds.

Economics of the fishermen themselves who were being displaced by these rules did enter into the consideration of the legislators and the commissioners who now had control of this thing. They certainly entered into their thinking and the economic impact it would have on their communities, Okeechobee and so forth. That's where the big battle was. I don't mean to overlook [Shellcracker Basin], but that's where the big battle was fought. And there was a very strong sportsmen's group in Gainesville. But they were not anticommercial fishermen.

JG: What did you conclude from your study of controlled seining?

Jack: Commercial fishing could be conducted under limitations without doing damage to recreational fishing. They had formal hearings or presentations at which they did their deliberations in order to enact rules and regulations. They acted to produce these resolutions here, which authorized a continuation of seining under certain restrictions and study systems and so forth. They changed their rules and policies a number of times since these days.

I became a thorn or the bump in the road that prevented them from carrying on their program of eliminating all commercial fishermen. And I was the impediment. I was the fall guy. I really was a lousy politician. I thought I tried to be a diplomat, but they replaced me with my assistant. He was not as militant as I was. Or else he had more sense than I had and realized that he didn't need to present those barricades.

I resigned, but the handwriting was on the wall. It came about when the new governor went in and the Florida Wildlife Federation Commission appointees became installed and got their power. They fired the old director and put their own director in who had been a sporting goods operator, and he became director and was for about six, ten months maybe. I was in his office one day and he said, "The Commission wants you to resign." I says, "Okay." I wasn't very happy, and I could see the handwriting on the wall. They were going to fire me if I didn't, because the five-man Commission now had a majority of three who maintained that my services should be discontinued.

JG: Do you believe it was because of your recommendations?

Jack: Oh sure. I became probably more of an advocate than I should have.

JG: You became political?

Jack: I guess you could say that. Yeah. I argued for what I thought was the truth of the matter, and that put me on the side of the commercial fishermen. I'm not sure that I did it, but anyway the perception was there. But I've been accused on both sides. I've been accused by commercial fishermen of favoring the sport fishermen, and vice versa. At any rate, I guess perception came that I was becoming more political than scientific.

You have no idea how hot some of these meetings got. At some of these hearings and public meetings, they had people [who] were called communist. I don't recall that any actual four-letter words were used, but it came mighty close to that.

JG: A fisheries biologist in Eustis replicated your study and came up with the same conclusions. Why isn't he going to get fired?

Jack: It's a different attitude today. And I like to think that I did quite a job of educating the fishermen of Florida, that it's not all black and white in this situation, or to recognizing that they do need facts on which to base this thing, and not just this emotional environment.

He [the new chief fisheries biologist] was instructed not to push as I had been pushing.

JG: How did you push? Did you use the media to your advantage?

Jack: I guess I did, yeah. I would invite news editors or outdoor writers to come out and witness our operations, what we were doing and how we were doing it. And naturally I'd try to give them a pitch at the same time. And I swayed a number of them. And some didn't need convincing. They just wanted more facts on which to be able to report.

JG: Was public relations built into your job description?

Jack: Wasn't supposed to be, but it had to be. That is one of the things that my experience taught the whole department, that you must pay attention to the public relations angle.

JG: You said earlier that things have changed. What has changed?

Jack: I don't think Marty [the fisheries biologist in Eustis] or his department are as strong advocates of putting into place the results of their research as I was expected to be in the time and atmosphere of the '40s and early '50s. In other words, I was expected to say which is the right thing to do, which is the wrong thing to do. I wasn't expected to present a set of sanitized facts. It was always, "And what is your opinion, Mr. Dequine, on what should be done in this case?" That's one reason. The other is, they're better educated in public relations than they were in those days. Furthermore, they have a lot more job protection. We had no protection. We were at the whim of a five-man commission.

JG: Was there direct pressure to get you out of the way?

Jack: Oh yes. That was one of Dan McCarty's campaign promises to this group [Florida Wildlife Federation] to get their support, to get rid of Jack Dequine. Now, Jane, I don't know that from my own personal knowledge, but this is what I was told by people who were in that political campaign—that McCarty promised John Clardy and some of the other members of that federation that he would see that I didn't stay.

JG: Did anyone talk about what would happen to the commercial fishing families?

Jack: It was only an issue. That is, it was unofficial. I got to know a lot of those people, and I could empathize. And I would mention it to the Commission and to these angry sportsmen about throwing these people out of work. Another thing that I was concerned with, showing up today, is the loss of skill. These people were skilled at what they did, and I watched these people over a period of years. I don't believe you could make up a competent seining crew, or at least not to the level of competence they had in those days.

JG: What was the response?

Jack: It depended on who you talked to. Members of the Commission who were general businessmen were usually pretty sympathetic, and they made that a consideration. Some of these red-hot sports fishermen would say, "Well, they're nothing but a bunch of outlaws, and they don't deserve any consideration."

JG: Why outlaws?

Jack: Some of them were. The Game Commission actually apprehended people transporting illegally caught fish out of Lake George or Lake Okeechobee across state lines into Georgia. Apprehended carloads of them. They ran them like the old bootleggers. They looked for a car that was weighted down in the back, and sure enough, a lot of them that they stopped had several hundred pounds of iced-down fish in the back of the car. So they were doing it.

When the '46 law went through, it was illegal to sell panfish: bluegill, shellcracker, crappie. But there was a good market for them in Georgia, so that's where they went. The fish dealer was getting around 26 to 31 cents a pound. Within a year after the ban, that price nearly doubled in the Georgia market. Getting up around 50 cents a pound or something like that. Like the old moonshiners.

In a report submitted in October of 1951 to the Commission, Dequine made a number of recommendations to address the problem of managing Florida's freshwater fisheries. He suggested:

1. Controlled commercial harvesting under strict and close supervision of GFC staff
2. Incorporation of a tagging system in which individual fish to be consumed in Florida would each be tagged, and containers of fish for export would also be tagged
3. Continuous study of the effect of commercial fishing and of sport fishing on Lakes Okeechobee and George, and establishment of an experimental lake for more intensive studies

4. An educational program to combat the uninformed emotionalism that drove the
   battle over commercial fishing
5. Financing of the supervisory program through the sale of tags and seals, or
   through a voluntary tax system providing for royalties to the state

Of these recommendations, Dequine wrote to the Commission:

> I am convinced that the legal sale at competitive prices of an abundant supply of bream
> and crappie from waters having a surplus of those species will be one of the most effec-
> tive methods of controlling the illegal take of those species from unapproved waters. The
> legal wholesale dealer will have an advantage over the illegal operator in being able to
> process and transport large poundages in bulk, and to give his customers a dependable
> source of supply of fresh fish without the risks and expenses incurred by the "bootlegger"
> in transporting small amounts to the present noncompetitive market.
>
> The demonstrated lack of damage to bass fishing and populations by regulated com-
> mercial operations, and the possible benefits to fishing inferred by the reputation enjoyed
> by Lake George and Lake Okeechobee during the years of commercial taking of bream
> and crappie, by the demonstrations of fishery workers in other areas, and by the consen-
> sus of opinion of fishery scientists over the entire United States, make the program of con-
> trolled harvesting of surplus bream and crappie a desirable approach to the problem of
> creating better bass fishing in these areas.

Recreational fishermen agreed to abide by the findings of Dequine's extensive
study until they learned the results. Dequine then sent the study to fisheries biologists
around the country for peer review. In response, a memorandum was sent to the GFC
"Director Coleman Newman and Members," dated May 7, 1951, and signed by the
executive vice president of the Sport Fishing Institute, the head of Game Fish and
Hatcheries in the U.S. Fish and Wildlife Service, the director of the Marine Laboratory at the University of Miami, and a fish culturist for Farm Ponds Laboratory of
the Alabama Polytechnic Institute. The writers endorsed Dequine's study:

> The conclusions drawn from this survey by Mr. Dequine are in accordance with the most
> recent and best works on fisheries management conducted elsewhere in the United States.
> If the Commission and the citizens of the State of Florida can agree that those water areas
> should be managed to produce the best sport fishing, then there can be no other conclu-
> sion but that sufficient regulated commercial fishing must be allowed to harvest ade-
> quately the rough fishes (catfish, shad, etc.) which compete with the sport fishes for food.
> This is essentially what a good farmer does; he removes the weeds so that the crop he
> wishes to grow may utilize the available food and space.

The position maintained by the fishermen of Shellcracker Haven, that their seining actually improved sport fishing through the removal of rough fish, found support
in Dequine's study of commercial fishing. Unfortunately, even if the GFC had resisted the political pressure of recreational fishers, it would have made no difference in
the ability of Shellcracker Haven's families to make a living. The GFC never con-
templated the continuation of commercial fishing with seines on the smaller lakes of
Florida, and an agency history published in its own magazine, *Florida Wildlife,* in
July of 1968, dismissed Dequine's findings. It reported instead that commercial fishing was found to be neither helpful nor harmful to the rough fish population. Politics
trumped science.

It was no less a bitter irony for the families of Shellcracker Haven when the GFC,
under the direction of Jack Dequine's assistant, Don Luethy, instituted a rough fish

control program to do exactly what the commercial fishers had done all along. While Luethy recognized in his proposal that such a program could provide the essential basis for reconciliation of commercial and recreational fishers, he did not believe its implementation using commercial fishermen was politically feasible.

With the loss of the preferred seining technology, commercial fishermen developed other innovative fishing strategies. Though none admitted doing it, Shellcracker Haven fishers knew about **monkey fishing,** a technique that spread rapidly and presented another enforcement problem for the GFC, costing the agency more than it intended to spend on personnel and equipment. Since monkey fishing was never among the GFC-permitted technologies, it was illegal.

A typical monkey machine, described by Luethy from observations of the GFC's confiscation collection, consisted of a hand-cranked telephone generator driven by a small direct-current motor, and powered by a six-volt car battery. (Earlier versions required the fishers to turn the crank themselves, a step that limited their catch in accordance with the fisher's endurance.) The output of the generator passes through a condenser to two extension cords that serve as electrodes. In operation, the fisher places one electrode in the water near the stern and one near the bow of the boat. Depth of the electrodes in the water has no obvious effect on the efficiency of the machine, but the use of a car battery to turn the telephone generator allowed fishermen to work until they got caught.

> The techniques of these illegal operators, along with social attitudes held by some of the local citizens, make for an almost impossible enforcement situation. To throw a monkey machine overboard to avoid arrest by a nearby wildlife officer would cost the violator only approximately $30.00, whereas he may often take as much as $50.00 worth of catfish in one night's operation.
>
> In more organized operations, the violators would transfer all of their machines into an exceptionally fast escape boat when approached by an officer. This flat-bottom, light boat driven by two high-horsepower kickers [motors] will outdistance the pursuing officers and then return to reissue the machines when the officers depart.
>
> In other cases, the violators will work in pairs, and when an officer approaches, they are pursued in a near lateral course. If the officer is able to overtake them, they throw the monkey machines in the adjacent boat. If the officer approaches the other boat, then it is thrown into the original boat. After a few flying transfers, then the machines are left in one boat and the sack, which previously contained the machines, is filled with a couple of bricks and thrown into the other boat. This boat in turn separates from his partner, and if the officers manage to apprehend this operator, they find bricks instead of evidence.
>
> These techniques, in addition to almost complete lack of convictions of the violators that were apprehended, create a demoralizing situation for the officers on duty in the area. For instance, since 1953, there have been thirteen (13) monkey fishing cases made in Putnam County, with only two convictions. There are approximately one hundred part or full-time "monkey" operators in the area. (Luethy 1956:17-18)

Luethy's study used confiscated machines and showed that "[t]here is no evidence that the monkey machines in their present stage of development capture or affect species of fishes other than catfishes." These machines were used all over the country in fish management programs when Luethy wrote that "the use of any of this type of apparatus by anyone but skilled technicians employed in fish management work is undesirable and vitally dangerous to the public interest." Then he translated his coded message:

Even though the current as normally used is not harmful to fish, the manner and methods of its application are so varied and potentially dangerous that without exceptionally tight controls, the practice has no place in a fisheries program. State and national surveys of fisheries values reveal such astounding figures when projected to the Florida sport fishing business, that in any real conflict between freshwater sports and commercial fishing, sports fishing must be given the primary consideration. The sports fishing industry must not be placed in jeopardy by a method of fishing as universally undesirable as uncontrolled "monkey fishing." (Luethy 1956)

Like midnight seining and bootlegging panfish to Georgia, monkey fishing represented another effort on the part of commercial fishers to provide for their families and maintain a traditional way of life. Luethy's assertion that monkey fishing was "universally undesirable" failed to consider that portion of the universe that desired it, and he ignored all values other than money, though it is also apparent that he placed value on the authority of the GFC. Valued livelihood traditions, even with the backing of empirical evidence, failed to affect the decision of the GFC whose new chief fisheries biologist identified sports fishing as the more lucrative and therefore more important constituency. Florida's fisheries management in the mid-1950s could be understood as the compromise between political and economic pressures and conservation.

The influx of tourists is recognized as the number one factor in the State's economic development, and fishing contributes a substantial impetus to this tourism.

[T]he economic and aesthetic values of sport fishing are recognized and accepted in present day society. It has become a part of the social structure of the nation. Its values far outweigh those of the fresh water commercial fisheries. Recognition of this situation has resulted in aggressive and widespread opposition by sports fishing interests to any real or assumed interference by commercial operations. Whether or not this concept is justified is beside the point. . . .

Commercial fisheries in the [Lake George] area contribute approximately one-third of fisheries revenue, whereas, sport fishing industries two-thirds. (Luethy 1956:8)

Luethy estimated the values of commercial and sport fisheries for Lake George and the "St. Johns River to Buffalo Bluff" area. He found that commercial fishing contributed 3.45 million pounds of catfish in 1955 worth $552,746. The sport fisheries contributed an estimated $2.4 million (based on projected expenditures of $11/fisher/day) plus an additional $30,183.25 in fishing licenses. But let's look more closely at these numbers.

Revenue for the two fishing sectors was calculated in different ways. Sport fishing revenue included money spent by fishers in lake community businesses as well as license fees collected by the GFC. These license fees included those for commercial fishers whose licenses were indistinguishable from those of recreational users. Furthermore, commercial fishing revenue only counted the value of the fish to fish dealers, who supplied the data and whose numbers Dequine believed to be artificially low. No accounting of the value of fish to commercial fishers, whom the GFC never counted, was made; nor was any consideration given to the effects of families' expenditures in area businesses, nor the further multiplication of value when retailers sold the catfish bought from commercial fishermen. In short, recreational calculations were inflated by the inclusion of commercial license fees and included a multiplier effect that commercial calculations omitted. It is no wonder that Dequine

Florida waters attract millions of recreational fishers every year.

expressed doubt about the oft-repeated argument that recreational fishing contributed more to Florida's economy than did commercial fishing.

The exclusive authority of the GFC to manage Florida's terrestrial and aquatic wildlife was further strengthened by the limitation placed on the state legislature to enact laws that would aid the Commission but would not be inconsistent with the regulations of the Commission. The Commission exercised both regulatory power and executive power in the area of planning, budgeting, personnel management, and purchasing. The authority to establish fees for permits or licenses to hunt and fish rested with the legislature, but the GFC received all revenue and used it for the purposes of management, protection, and conservation. This directly tied the number of licenses or permits sold and the exercise of police power to the agency's budget, and this relationship tied the agency to its recreational constituency.

GOING GREAT GUNS

Recreational hunters and fishers, who argued that commercial users were all outlaws, pressed hard for increased enforcement of GFC rules and regulations. Their direct and indirect contributions, representing 94% of the agency's total revenue in 1941, financed expansion of the agency as a whole and allowed for development in particular areas, especially law enforcement. Beginning in 1947, the year Ben Morgan took over as director, the GFC appropriated 72% of its annual budget to this cause. In the 1948 biannual report (GFC 1949), law enforcement is described as "the biggest and perhaps the most important" among agency divisions. Money spent for its development went for 124 jeeps, 160 outboard motorboats, 150 horse and boat trailers, 4 airboats, 9 powerboats, and 2 airplanes. More enforcement personnel were hired as well. The number of officers rose to 228 in December of 1948, up 33% from

171 officers employed in January of 1947. These officers received pay raises to attract younger and more capable people to replace the "deadwood" who, "it was found, were not qualified to perform the duties of a wildlife officer. Many had received their jobs solely through political patronage and made no effort to earn the salaries they received" (GFC 1949:64).

The new force also received uniforms for the first time, dignifying the enforcement branch and noticeably boosting employee morale. They acquired ranks like those of the military such as captains, lieutenants, and sergeants, with each having supervisory authority over a given number of men. In the field, uniformed wildlife officers, authorized to carry firearms and enforce all the laws assigned to other police officers, presented the public face of the new, high-powered GFC. In 1980, the writer of the agency's annual report described the Division of Law Enforcement as "the sentinel charged with safeguarding this wildlife treasure from those who would selfishly abuse it" (GFC 1980:12). Today, these officers wear holsters that are specially designed to keep anyone from taking their weapons, bulletproof vests, two-way radios that enable them to stay in contact with their headquarters, and semiautomatic shoulder weapons.

Over the first two years of its existence, the law enforcement division made 5,357 arrests of which 91% resulted in conviction. About 68% of these arrests dealt with violations of freshwater fishing rules. Another 30% involved violation of game laws. By 1956, the budget share going to law enforcement had dropped to 54%, and in 1991 that share represented 43%. For fiscal year 2002–03, enforcement accounted for 34% of the total agency budget.

The proportional decline in these appropriations obscures the dramatic increases that have occurred annually. It also hides the strict discipline of Florida's population over the years, resulting from an expanded enforcement branch and growing numbers of arrests. From its 1947 budget of $640,500, law enforcement received more than $22 million in 1991. By fiscal year 2002–03, the figure had risen to $73.6 million. This figure represents real increases in the agency's investment in enforcement: The 1947 budget allocation in 2001 dollars would have been only $5.6 million. These expenditures have consistently represented the largest annual investment of the FWC, which today employs state-of-the-art equipment and a highly trained enforcement staff to carry out its expanded responsibilities. The agency currently oversees 672 species of wildlife, 208 species of freshwater fish, and over 500 saltwater species. Wildlife officers patrol "over 37 million acres of public and private land, 8,246 miles of tidal coastline, 12,000 miles of rivers and streams, 3 million acres of lakes and ponds, and 11,000 miles of canals" (FWC 2003b).

To carry out this daunting responsibility, the FWC has expanded the number of wildlife officers in the field who, in fiscal year 2001–02, worked some 800,000 hours in preventive patrol and investigations. The law enforcement program accounts for just under half (891 employees) of all agency staff (1,819), of whom over 350 are field officers (personal communication). During the fiscal year 1990–91, officers issued 20,324 citations and 9,999 warnings (GFC 1992). This record reflects the modern structure of the agency, which now employs, in addition to uniformed wildlife officers who act as a wilderness police force, a 24-hour toll-free telephone reporting system (Wildlife Alert) for citizens to report violators for rewards of $50 to $1,000. Plainclothes wildlife detectives conduct covert undercover operations in areas and situations where uniformed officers and marked vehicles would be at a disadvantage; aerial patrols conduct surveillance; and wildlife inspectors regulate trade in wildlife. Ten "K-9" units, dogs trained in wildlife detection, also work around the state. These dogs are trained to follow both wildlife and human scents and are used in investigations and search-and-rescue missions.

All sworn wildlife officers go through a 750-hour training program in which they learn all police and commission enforcement skills from searches and arrests to surveillance and firearm retention. In addition to the law enforcement division's responsibility to protect fish and wildlife resources, the division is also charged with maintenance of public order during natural disturbances and civil emergencies, and assisting local and state law enforcement agencies. When the Pope visited Miami, the GFC contributed to security provision alongside Miami police officers.

FLACK CONTROL

The Commission saw its enforcement personnel as the front line of public relations. Officers received training in how to conduct themselves in the courtroom and in the field from University of Florida professors, wildlife specialists, public relations specialists, "and well-known law enforcement officers" (GFC 1949:68). Between 1947 and 1949, the agency set aside funds specifically for public relations, although money had been spent for "information and education" as early as 1941. Beginning in 1950, public relations became part of the expanded information and education budget. Dequine's successor articulated the lessons in public relations learned by the GFC:

> In considering the public relations viewpoint in regard to any matter, it should be remembered that the important thing is the impression that the general public has of the particular matter in question. In considering public relations, it should be remembered that it is not important what a thing actually is—but it is important what the thing appears to be. (Luethy 1956:12)

From the public rancor of the GFC in the 1940s and 1950s, the FWC has come a long way. The Office of Informational Services (OIS) manages the agency's image using various public relations tools: the popular magazine *Florida Wildlife,* environmental education, hunter educational programs, news releases, brochures, posters, an extensive Web site, and an electronic newsletter. The agency's public relations arm was one of the first in the country to develop a marketing program for nature-based activities. Among their marketing activities is work with the private sector to take advantage of the economic value of fish and wildlife (FWC 2003b).

So keen is the FWC's awareness of its public image that, according to a fisheries biologist, the agency sometimes makes decisions that have no harmful or beneficial effect on the species in question, but which favorably affect the public's view of the agency. The example given by this biologist dealt with the setting of bag limits:

> Biologically, in the state of Florida, for the most part except for maybe the large-mouth bass and some other predators, there's no biological reason for bag limits. But since the normal person cannot go out there and catch his limit anyhow, we felt like this would be a good public relations tool. So we established what we feel are generous bag limits, especially for panfish. You know, you can catch fifty panfish in aggregate, and very few people do. If we can use public relations in our favor, it would be expedient for us.

When recreational fishers blamed commercial fishers for declining catches, they not only pushed for laws and enforcement, but also for freshwater restocking of sport fish. Research told fisheries biologists that restocking was at best a short-term solution when the problem could be located in changes in a lake or river's carrying capacity, but the political demands of the agency's largest constituency won out over science again. The fisheries biologist provided an example:

> We were going through a period of time where the lakes were in degraded conditions as the result of over**eutrophication,** and we had habitats degraded with muck buildup and disappearance of vegetation. And we had manipulation of the population on a natural basis, so they automatically figured the answer is to stock fish.
>
> What we tried to do was to educate them that you could stock all the fish you want to, and with the holding capacities of the lakes like they are, it wouldn't do any good. I've spent the last four or five years with some stocking evaluations where we actually took some lakes and tried to manipulate the population of the lakes by stocking and stayed right on top of it. And, as a result, we showed actually, because we were able to mark our fingerling fish with a magnetic tagging device, that we didn't change the population one whit.
>
> So we tried to teach them that the perceived problem is not always the real problem.

THE FLORIDA FISH AND WILDLIFE CONSERVATION COMMISSION

The constitutionality of the GFC withstood innumerable tests, including attempts by the state legislature to regulate freshwater fishing, similar county and city efforts, an attempt by the legislature to remove certain salty waters from GFC control, and a legislative effort to place the GFC under the control of the Department of Natural Resources. In a new state constitution (passed in 1968 and amended in 1973), Article IV, Section 9, gave maximum breadth to the Commission's authority, described as "the non-judicial powers of the state with respect to wild animal life and fresh water aquatic life."

The passage of the constitutional amendment that created the GFC had far-reaching effects on resource management and on the agency itself. Dequine's story highlights the major changes in Florida's resource management culture: dramatic growth in the size and influence of the recreational constituency; availability to the GFC of a reliable money supply; incorporation of scientific research into species management; enforcement improvement and expansion of agency authority; and greater attention paid to public relations. As Luethy said, "It is not important what a thing actually is—but it is important what the thing appears to be."

CATFISH FARMS, SPORTS FISHING, AND SHELLCRACKER HAVEN TODAY

Today, catfish farms are pushing out commercial freshwater fishing. These capital-intensive businesses control quality and quantity of production. They also wage successful marketing campaigns that claim that farm-fed catfish are healthier and taste better than wild catfish. The result is that grocers and restaurants increasingly prefer farm-fed catfish, and the prices offered for wild catfish have fallen. Small-scale, local market production and low prices have kept Shellcracker Haven incomes low and

A lucky catch

have, thus far, also conserved wild catfish populations for future harvests. But the only responses fishing families can make to compensate for low prices is to intensify production by putting out more trotlines (a response limited by available labor) or find another line of work to try to keep up with the rising cost of living. Ironically, the sports fishing industry has offered some options.

A national survey found that in 2001, 3.1 million people fished in Florida an average of over fifteen days each, and they spent $5.3 billion doing it (U.S. Fish and Wildlife Service 2002). Growth in tourism in the Shellcracker Basin has stimulated a market for special fishing baits, particularly for those who come to Red's and the few other remaining fish camps that operate in small towns around the lakes. In addition to sports fishers vacationing in the region, the increasing popularity of bass tournaments has opened up this income-earning opportunity. Bait fishers seine the shallows of Shellcracker Lake and other lakes nearby for freshwater shrimp and a popular baitfish called **shiners.** Shiners are small, silvery fish whose marketability is seasonally limited by their sensitivity to heat. When temperatures are cool or cold, selling shiners becomes most profitable.

Red's manager, Mr. Marsh, claims to have bought as many as twenty to thirty dozen shiners per day at $5 to $6 per dozen when business was good. He sold them at a profit, netting himself anywhere from $40 to $150 day, before the severe drought that caused lake levels to drop too low for anyone to launch boats from his ramp.

With such potential income from the sale of shiners, many people who lived around Shellcracker Basin Lakes competed to sell their catch. Only a few arranged regular sales, and these came at their customers' mostly irregular discretion. Among the more successful competitors were three members of the Knight family, who subsidized their separate household incomes with sales of shiners. Six fish camps, several independent bait shops, and a few tour guides bought these fish from Shellcracker Haven producers in the late 1980s. Then drought and aquatic weed infestations forced most lake-dependent businesses to close their doors.

By January of 1990, Red's was also suffering, so Mr. Marsh bought only ten dozen shiners at a time, and he did not buy them every day. Income for bait producers, whose production was already seasonally limited, dropped from $100 to $180 per day to between $50 and $60 on the days Mr. Marsh bought shiners. Members of the Knight family had to increase work in other areas to compensate for this loss.

Mr. Knight's brother-in-law "Dan" operates a bait business in freshwater shrimp. His business, like others in Shellcracker Haven, depends for its success on family labor, and on demand for shrimp. Shrimping has been difficult because, as Dan explained, Shellcracker Lake is no longer the healthy resource for abundant shrimp that it once was, so he must pay the additional cost to look elsewhere. The implication for him undoubtedly parallels the problem presented others for whom Shellcracker Lake can no longer provide a livelihood. The cost of pulling a boat to more distant lakes and the locally reduced demand for bait have cut into the profitability of the business. He, too, must compensate by increasing other kinds of work.

While families in Shellcracker Haven adjust to changing resource availability in the basin where they live, the state agency that oversees those resources takes a view that assesses the need for species management decisions for the state as a whole. In 1998, a new constitutional amendment changed the agency's name again and expanded its authority over fish and wildlife. Under the newly created Florida Fish and Wildlife Conservation Commission (the FWC), saltwater fisheries and freshwater fisheries have been brought, with terrestrial wildlife, under the same agency umbrella. But greater authority, it turns out, does not translate into greater conservation of Florida's diverse wild species.

According to the 2001 program evaluation and justification review, 261 of 532 (49.1%) terrestrial species and 46 of 126 (29.1%) freshwater fish species are suspected or known to be in decline (OPPAGA 2001:7-12). In spite of good science, public relations sophistication, well-armed and dedicated game wardens, constitutional status, and seemingly unassailable legal authority, the FWC has been unable to stop habitat loss, its degradation, and pollution related to development activities because these occur beyond the scope of agency authority. Alligators have appeared on the list of species threatened by Florida development. The next chapter addresses their place in FWC management, and in the livelihoods of Shellcracker Haven families, and it will direct us to consider questions concerning the future of Florida's biodiversity and rural communities.

4/Gators, Gator Hunters, and the FWC

This is the first legal gator I ever got.

(Voice off-camera)

Them that's on the hill ought to stay on the hill.

—*Buck*

It was the alligator hunting that first attracted me to Shellcracker Haven. I grew up where reptiles were small and shy and most often slithering hastily away as they fled my aggressive curiosity. So I felt awe at the sight of Florida's largest and most ancient reptiles. Soon after our move to "the sunshine state," my husband, children, and I made it a habit to walk to Lake Alice where, in the heat of the day, alligators lay on the bank like oversized, drugged lizards. Signs posted by the dock read, "Don't feed the alligators," yet visitors and students wandered casually around the lake edge and within mere feet of powerful jaws. We kept a healthy distance from the large predators that, like us, occupied the top of their food chain, until we heard someone shout, "There's a nest over here!" We could not resist the opportunity to see our first alligator nest up close.

"Oh, look! That must be its mother," I said, appreciating the warmth of her protective presence. My little one stepped closer to the water where "Mom" looked on. She showed us no more than her snout and eyes, leaving the rest of her leathered body to lie comfortably in the soft muck of the lake bottom. As is the case with many species, female alligators are smaller than **bull gators,** but they tend to ferocity when their young are threatened. We forgot that as we admired the heap of grass and brush that held her unhatched babies.

The mother alligator appeared to recede a bit into the water. Then suddenly, with no other warning, she lunged, seeming to hurl herself in a tidal wave at my little girl. Joanie screamed at a pitch I was sure had never been heard by either alligators or humans as we raced away from the threat. Much to our surprise and relief, the mother alligator never even left the lake, knowing in some primeval way that her display had been sufficient to protect her young. I did not forget her when the opportunity arose to study her species' only predators, alligator hunters, some of whom live on Shellcracker Lake.

The reptilian order *Crocodylia* includes alligators and crocodiles, and it represents some of the most valuable and heavily traded species in international commerce. Among these are saltwater crocodiles (*Crocodylus porosis*), New Guinea crocodiles (*C. novaeguineae*), Nile crocodiles (*C. niloticus*), and *Alligator Mississippiensis,* also known as the American Alligator.

Alligators have attained totemic status in Florida. The "Fightin' Gators" football team of the University of Florida in Gainesville constructs its image from associations with alligators' powerful, aggressive characteristics, and some alumni bear the title "bull gators" for their support of the team. Inside the football stadium, called "the swamp," fans "do the gator chomp." Bumper stickers read, "If you ain't a Gator . . . you must be Gator Bait." Local businesses also use alligator caricatures to sell their products, and postcards link erotica to exotica on Florida beaches where bronzed sunbathers pose with open-mouthed alligators.

In addition to the comic-strip world of sports team mascots and tourist kitsch, alligators symbolize what remains of wild, primeval Florida. Ironically, those images used to attract visitors to the state undermine the longevity of the attraction as visitors become permanent residents whose own habitat requirements eliminate or degrade all other species' habitats. Conflicts result when two top-feeding species try to inhabit the same space, so alligator hunting has returned to Florida.

The Alligator Management Program (AMP) brings together the FWC tradition as a hunting organization, its extensive experience in law enforcement and public relations, and a theoretical and biological sophistication that has made it a model for other nations. The program's first coordinator and contributor to program development identified the two principles that explain the agency's policy decisions. He said, "We do whatever is biologically sound and politically possible" (personal communication).

In achieving this compromise, the AMP models more than program elements and organization. It incorporates the underlying assumptions of the particular worldview mentioned earlier—coupling conservation of species to free markets and assigning value based on economics. It maintains the separation of culture from nature, that is, of people from the natural world within which they live and on which they depend. The AMP accepts that hierarchical relationships will be imposed if they do not exist, or taken for granted if they do. Ecosystem constituents with greater commercial value are more likely to be conserved; the needs of people are more important than the needs of other species; and the power of some people over others is right and proper. Such beliefs can lead to the establishment of an adversarial relationship between those people who need access to a managed species and those with the power to withhold that access.

The AMP links some Shellcracker Haven households to the international market for **exotic leathers** and so has the potential to deepen local interest in the health of alligator habitat. The problem is that habitats for all wild species in Florida are shrinking or are being degraded by development and pollution, and the legislature sees these threats as lying outside the scope of FWC authority. The question then is this: Can alligators and their habitats be conserved if those authorized to conserve them have no authority to address the causes of their decline, and if those who live near alligators and have vested interests in the health of their habitats become detached? What if, as in the case of freshwater fisheries, politics contradict what is biologically sound?

EARLY MARKETS

Kersey (1975) examined many hide buyers' ledgers compiled between 1870 and 1930. He found that buyers bought mostly from Native Americans, and he estimated that during the 1800s, one buyer in the Big Cypress area bought an average of 5,000 hides per month. He also found participation in the international skin trade: a trapper contracted to deliver 5,000 hides to a Paris leather company. Alligator skin had occupied a prestigious, international position among exotic leathers for two centuries, but it was not until 1979 that sale of alligator meat became legal (GFC 1987).

Until 1943, the year the GFC outlawed freshwater seining, alligator hunting in the state of Florida was legal and unregulated. That year saw a dramatic drop in the reported harvest: 190,000 skins reported in 1929 and 6,800 skins reported in 1943 (Allen and Neill 1949). In response, the GFC closed the breeding season and prohibited the taking of any alligator smaller than four feet in length. This approach represented the management standard until 1962: Seasonal regulation and size limitations were determined primarily by the intuition of biologists, wildlife officers, administrators, environmental groups, and legislators (Woodward and Delany 1987).

Personnel at the GFC believed the alligator population rebounded between 1942 and 1945 as a result of this protection, and in 1954, they imposed a six-foot size limit. The agency also began to keep harvest records that they believed showed declining alligator populations. At that point, in 1962, they banned hunting altogether.

Hines (1979) reviewed these records and noted the incomplete reporting on which conclusions were based. He also pointed out that during the 1950s and 1960s, considerable wetland drainage occurred and marsh vehicles improved. These together limited the natural protection available to alligators in large **wetland** areas.

The U.S. Fish and Wildlife Service added alligators to the endangered species list in 1967, and by the early 1970s, population growth became apparent, the number of complaints about alligators rose, and attacks on humans increased (Woodward and Delany 1987). Between 1948 and 1959, the GFC recorded four unprovoked attacks on people. Between 1959 and 1972, they recorded six attacks. Then in the early 1970s, between two and five attacks were reported each year, with an unusual high of fourteen attacks in 1977, one of which resulted in the death of a man in Charlotte County.

Illegal trapping continued throughout this period, and prices trappers received for their hides, like bootlegged panfish and moonshine, continued to rise. Hines (1979) reported that some trappers received $7 per foot in 1965, although most received between $5 and $5.50. Because of the illegality of the activity being documented, Hines acknowledged that conclusions drawn from GFC files would have to be considered carefully. He estimated from these records that Florida trappers sold 140,000 hides between 1965 and 1971, and that these data, in combination with overall size composition of harvested hides, demonstrated that alligators were not endangered. Today, Florida's alligator program managers agree with these conclusions.

Passage of the Lacey Act in 1971 effectively stopped the black market in alligator hides by prohibiting their interstate shipment (GFC 1989). By the mid-1970s, as nuisance complaints reached 4,000 to 5,000 annually and the legislative infusion of money made research possible, the GFC surveyed the population and argued for reclassification of the species. In 1977, alligators moved off of the endangered list of **CITES,** the Convention on International Trade in Endangered Species of Wild Fauna and Flora, and onto the CITES list of threatened species. This change enabled the GFC, in 1978, to implement the statewide **Nuisance Alligator Control Program (NACP)** (Woodward and Delany, 1987) and to hire Mr. Knight as a nuisance trapper.

Mr. Knight, the best known among Shellcracker Haven's alligator trappers, told me that he began hunting gators as a teenager. He modestly denied his reputation as "one of the best."

> **Mr. K.:** I don't know about that, but I'll tell you what. Me and Buck done some hunting. When everybody else was failing to get gators, me and him would get us three or four every night. There was some professionals out there, too—that supposed to have been— one guy by the name of [O.S.]. He's supposed to have been one of the gooder hunters there was in this country, you know. And he'd go out there, and me and Buck, we'd get three or four gators in a night, and he wouldn't get nary, and he couldn't understand how we was doing it. But it was luck, that's all, luck. It ain't skill. Lot of people thinks it's skill, but it was just luck.
>
> **JG:** Can you tell me a little about yourself, about how you got started gator hunting?
>
> **Mr. K.:** Well I just started alligator hunting when I was about 17 years old, or 16 years old, and I been doing it off and on. Only when it was illegal—they was on the extinct list—I hunted up until then. They permitted us back then, had to have a permit to take them, had to take six foot and up. Couldn't take anything under six foot. Then when they went on the endangered list, I put a application in with the state when they started the nuisance hunt and was lucky enough to get hired. I been with them ever since '77. I went to work February 1977 for the state.
>
> My wife's daddy, I watched him skin when we was kids, and my daddy, I watched him skin. And I knew it had to be real tedious because, if you cut holes in the hide, that's a third of the price off, so you don't want to lose a third of the price of your hides for sure. You just have to show them what's what. Just be careful. When anybody first starts skinning, it just takes a lot of patience really when you start off. It ain't a fast job. You can't just jump in there and just whack, whack, whack—because if you do, you mess the hide up.
>
> **JG:** What was the market like before the state restricted hunting?
>
> **Mr. K.:** You had buyers that come around, same buyers that's buying now, see. Plott Fur and Hide bought most of our hides back then, out of Georgia, and they come around generally once a week. They had a man come around to buy hides, or once every two weeks, or else they had a man in Ocala and a man in Leesburg that bought for them. And if you had a I.D., you could carry them to either one of those buyers and he'd buy your hide.
>
> It was just alike, hide and fur. Fur buyers, same ones bought our hides, too. We didn't get anything for them. I think just before they stopped us, we'd get $5 a foot for them. Anything that was up to seven foot. Anything seven and a half, eight foot up, they buttoned on us, see. They'd say, "Well, he's buttoned. I can't give you nothing but half." So that's two dollars and a half a foot. They got that alligator two dollars and a half a foot!

"Buttons" are osteoderms, or bony growths, in the hide that reduce its price. Mr. Knight made it clear that hide buyers felt no obligation to show evidence of these flaws, and trappers had no leverage with which to negotiate.

JG: With prices so low, why did you hunt alligators?

Mr. K.: I frog hunted. I had a airboat and I'd frog hunt. And when I'd run up on a alligator, I'd always just get him just to help out right along. A dollar's a dollar, whichever way you made it, you know.

With such vulnerability to the greed of hide buyers, the Knights would come to appreciate state regulation of alligator hunting, even though state intervention in seining had all but destroyed their livelihoods.

Mr. K.: They had you, you know. It wasn't like it is now. I mean, now we got control of it where we can do something with it, with our hides. We can take [their bid] if we want to sell them. If we don't want to take their bid, we don't have to. But back then, you didn't have no option, you know, because all your buyers was the same way. All of them come around, give you near nothing for them. It was the same way with furs, the same way.

JG: How did you get control of the market?

Mr. K.: We didn't until the Game Commission took it over. The first year that we tried to sell hides, we was offered $5. I take that back. We sold a very few hides to a company out of the Carolinas, bought our hides. They gave us $17 or $18 a foot. Then afterwards, we didn't sell any. When they did bid, they offered us $5 a foot and we no-saled them. Finally they offered $9 a foot, and we sold them. The Game Commission cut down their percentage this time because we didn't get nothing for them. They was good to us on that deal.

Others I spoke to could find no silver lining in the state's presence. When the GFC began regulating the "taking" of alligators, some trappers resisted and became, from a legal standpoint, poachers. A trapper in Shellcracker Haven told me how he hunted alligators at night, took them into the weeds to skin them, and abandoned the carcass, including the meat, at the site. He then arranged a meeting with a hide buyer who had total control over the illegal sale.

ALLIGATOR MANAGEMENT TODAY

The AMP includes the Nuisance Alligator Control Program (NACP), a Private Lands program, alligator farming, and the statewide alligator hunt on public waters. The agency describes the AMP as "the means of managing alligators on a sustained-yield basis while recognizing them as an ecologically, aesthetically, and economically valuable resource" (FWC 2002b).

Unique to the AMP is a special conceptualization of conservation known by program managers as **value-added conservation (VAC).** Value-added conservation is a theory that those with a vested interest in a resource will work to conserve it. Promotional literature for alligator products emphasizes the conservation aspects of the harvest and reproduces a statement of VAC:

> Environmentally-aware consumers will only want products from legal and protected renewable resources. American alligator will be a more preferred leather product. . . . It is one of the most valuable exotic leathers in the world and its conservation success story is a classic example of modern wildlife management.
>
> Conservation through utilization is a management strategy that is working with the alligator in Florida, Louisiana and other southern states. . . . The idea of protecting and yet harvesting the same species may seem a contradiction. How can you save something and harvest it too?

The answer is simple. The "economic incentive" to manage a wildlife species like the alligator provides the strongest argument for maintaining the natural wetlands it needs to survive. That natural habitat will then provide wetlands to other animal species too. If a harvest is based on scientific facts and only a fraction of the renewable resource is taken, then the management of the resource becomes a powerful incentive to protect both the species and their habitats. (Florida Department of Agriculture and Consumer Services:n.d.)

The coordinator of the AMP offered some anecdotal evidence in support of the theory of VAC. He told me that during the experimental hunts, Owens-Illinois, the same company from earlier Shellcracker Haven history, proposed the construction of a condominium community on the shore of Shellcracker Lake. Those residents who hunted alligators there argued before the county commission that such a project would damage the lake's alligator population, and the project was scrapped. (We'll return to this story in the last chapter.)

The AMP proposal states that "the foremost reason for implementing an operational alligator management program is to benefit the alligator resource and its habitat in Florida." Decisions concerning kinds or levels of harvest would therefore be based on actions construed "to result in the greatest long-term benefit to the resource." These benefits, in accord with the theory of VAC, were to be measured two ways:

1. The economic values providing direct economic incentives to conserve alligators
2. The development of a broad constituency who are most likely to vigorously support wetland preservation and enhancement

These criteria show that the FWC believes that the prices "industry participants" receive for their products will relate to their interest in conserving wetlands and alligators, and that these interests will be transformed into political activity as needed. The list of industry participants includes nuisance hunters, trappers, meat and hide processors, farmers, participating private wetland owners, tanners, brokers, formal organizations of any of these groups, producers of finished products, and all employees who rely on any of these.

Here are some important questions we might ask about VAC as a management tool:

- How does the program benefit different participant groups?
- How are benefits distributed? Will it matter to long-term program success that trappers, meat and hide processors, farmers, tanners, and fashion designers benefit differently and do not share equally in program benefits?
- Is an effective constituency developed through program components? Are the interests in protecting a small lake in Shellcracker Basin the same for a tanner of exotic hides and a trapper who, with his family, lives in the house built by his children's grandparents at the lake's edge? Will the Miami sports hunter who was selected by lottery to hunt on Shellcracker Lake attend meetings in a distant county that concern the lake's health?

The components of the AMP are described in the text that follows. All of these affect the families of Shellcracker Haven.

The Nuisance Alligator Control Program (NACP)

Alligators rarely attack humans who have not provoked them, but they do attack and eat domestic livestock and pets, damage commercial fishing equipment, and create traffic hazards when they cross roads (Woodward and David 1994). When they do attack people, especially in the unusual cases where death results, Florida newspapers have a field day. The death of a little girl in 1988 even made the national news.

When species numbers rebounded in the 1970s and nuisance complaints grew to some 5,000 per year, the GFC found itself in the difficult position of simultaneously working to facilitate species recovery while protecting public safety. Out of several management options considered, the GFC determined that subcontracting with trappers would be the most cost-effective approach.

I heard the same story twice. A GFC staff member, with Mr. Knight by his side, was charged with conducting interviews for the hiring of nuisance trappers. The staff member called in one of the applicants. The trapper, described as "an old cracker," really wanted the job. He said, "I really love hunting gators. In fact, there ain't nothing I like better in the whole world than hunting gators, not even sex." Mr. Knight reportedly looked him over rather closely and responded, "I guess one of us is doing something wrong."

The Knights' future in the AMP was set in motion through the Nuisance Alligator Control Program. This program helped finance the costs of upgrading their processing facilities, an investment that virtually ensured some income for the family every year. For the GFC, in addition to the revenue hides provided, the program brought the state and its involvement in alligator management face-to-face with Florida citizens in a positive way, and it constituted the first stage of learning how to manage the human component of the AMP.

During the early years of the nuisance program, the GFC observed production of hides on a small scale. They contracted with 50 trappers around the state and monitored them closely. This careful scrutiny involved tracking skins and meat, observing trapper activities, and biologists' meetings, one-on-one, with trappers to discuss experiences and observations. By marketing the hides for trappers, the GFC learned what hide buyers expected, and they learned how to stop illegal hide sales.

The GFC learned most of what it needed to know about managing hide production and marketing by observation and interviewing, and by engaging in the activity themselves. They became **participant observers.** When it came to learning about meat marketing, they relied much more heavily on their informants to teach them the ropes, or the potential loopholes through which illegal marketing could occur. The AMP's coordinator told me how they learned and developed the program:

> On the meat sales, it was an interactive process. What do you need to sell meat; what do we need in terms of record keeping; what kind of record is it feasible for you to keep? We always started out real restrictive and worked our way down to where we saw a balance. . . . We always started out closing every loophole that we would anticipate or that we would see.

Mr. Knight's son remembers conversations with AMP managers in which they considered all the ways the young Knight would go about subverting the legal system. The Knights understood well the benefits of working with the GFC, and they had years of experience dealing alone and from a subordinate position with wily hide buyers. They fully supported intervention into the market by the state in hopes of improving their lot. I estimated average annual economic benefits to their families of participation in the nuisance control program and experimental harvests between 1984 and 1988 at $41,500. Divided by three households, and less the cash earnings of a granddaughter, each household earned a little over $12,000 per year from hide and meat sales. Among other things, that money went to repair equipment and a washing machine, to buy clothes, and to pay for a trip to a dentist. These benefits only reinforced the importance to the family of its ties to a tradition of hunting and fishing and to the agency that controlled many aspects of that life.

Nuisance trappers like Mr. Knight, who retired in 1991, are not state employees. By subcontracting with them, trappers pay the costs of alligator removal and ideally recover these through sales of the hide and meat. Some years are better than others, and because hide prices have dropped in recent years, the FWC has considered alternatives to help maintain trappers' incentives to work in the NACP.

When an alligator dives into a swimming pool, takes up residence in a golf course pond, or behaves in any way or place a person considers a problem, the concerned citizen can call the FWC toll-free. If questions arise about the validity of the complaint, a wildlife officer or biologist might go to the site to assess the situation. If the alligator is over 1.2 meters and the complaint has merit, the agency relays the necessary information and issues a special permit to the area nuisance trapper. The trapper goes to the designated location and searches for the offending alligator. If he finds it, he removes the animal and usually kills it out of the public eye. Fewer than half of the nuisance permits issued are actually filled because the problem alligators are found to be too small, are not found at all, or cannot be trapped (Woodward and Cook 2000).

What constitutes a nuisance? The FWC has size and situation criteria, but not everyone agrees. Mr. Knight and his son arrived at a system of house-lined canals off a small lake where two large alligators had been sighted. Some residents felt concerned about the nearness of the sharp-toothed carnivores whose diet, it is popularly repeated, consists of small dogs, preferably poodles, and children. While carrying out the search, an elderly resident surprised Mr. Knight when she swam by. This, she explained to her alarmed observers, was her daily routine, to swim out of the canals into the lake and back into the canals every evening. Mr. Knight reminded her that alligators begin feeding around dusk and that she would not stand a chance in the water against a hungry male. He lost a finger to an 11.5-foot alligator that weighed in at about 600 pounds. He mistakenly thought his son had killed it. He described the event:

> Well, we just went over on the highway that morning about 2 or 2:30. My son went on and shot him, and I just reached down to get him, and he caught me. I reached to catch him, and that was it! It was so quick. Yeah, the deputies was upset, too. They took off.

At the canals that day, Mr. Knight and his son failed in their attempt to find the nuisance gators they sought. They went on home, worrying about the safety of the woman they had seen swimming in the canals.

Private Lands Alligator Management Program (PLAMP)

Wetland management has become a highly sensitive subject in the United States, particularly in Florida where the second Bush administration's redefinition of a "wetland" has now reduced the total area protected by law. As an example of how sensitive this issue is, under the first Bush administration, when redefinition was proposed without success, the agency changed the wording of the rules from "wetland habitat" to "alligator habitat." The change was designed to appease private landowners who regarded the program survey requirement as a back-door attempt to find out how much wetland they owned. Though no accurate assessment of the state's wetland area exists, of the estimated 50% remaining since drainage began in the late 1800s (Myers and Ewel 1990), large tracts are believed to exist on the millions of acres owned by private companies.

Through the PLAMP, the FWC offers financial incentives to preserve wetlands by allowing landowners to sell the rights to a harvest of alligators. Landowners may lease large tracts to hunters or alligator farmers in exchange for a privately negotiated fee. Additionally, "trophy" alligators, those of unusual size whose processing involves taxidermy, can be worth upwards of $2,000 each to a landowner.

The rules of the program require certification by a wildlife biologist of wetland inventories, including aerial surveys of alligator nests and nightlight counts of alligators. (Alligators are active at night and are counted when light is reflected back from their eyes.) Landowners or those with leases of 1,000 acres of alligator habitat or an estimated minimum of 100 alligators greater than four feet may qualify for program permits. (There are some exceptions.) License holders may take alligators greater than nine feet (all males) and those under six feet from April 1 through August 31, and nonhatchling alligators from September 1 through March 31. Landowners can also make habitat available for the gathering of eggs and hatchlings to be "grown out" by alligator farmers.

The Knights, with the help of Tommy Hines, a former FWC biologist whose work was cited earlier, leased 22,000 acres from a timber company. Hines made the contacts for the Knights, performed the aerial survey for $40 (a fraction of the usual cost), performed the nightlight counts with no charge instead of the usual $600, and supplied the necessary certification to secure a harvest quota. For the assistance of another experienced and proficient hunter, Hines, now a wildlife entrepreneur, also paid Mr. Knight's grandson a wage to work with him.

Often, because of the costs to the user, participants represent wealthy trophy hunters. I met one such man in the Knight's shed where they provided customized processing of the trophy-end of a large alligator. The hunter belonged to Safari International and already claimed a highly diverse collection of trophies from other parts of the world. Hines guided the successful hunt, as he did many others, for fees that ranged between $600 and $800.

In an effort to learn about corporate participation in the PLAMP, I interviewed the manager of a large property owned by a multinational pulp and paper corporation. The coordinator of the AMP had told me that land planted to pines generates up to ten times more earnings than a wetland of equal acreage from which alligators could be harvested. I asked the company manager how his superiors would make a decision to participate in the AMP instead of draining habitat and planting pines. The manager's response was as simple as my question. The company would make its decision based solely on the question of profits. I thought it might not always be that simple, in part because the AMP coordinator had mentioned borderline cases where the money might be about equal between investment in pines and investment in alligator habitat. If the company wanted the bonus of association with wetland conservation—and I knew public image to be the Achilles heel of business—decisions might be made favoring alligator habitat. On the other hand, when Georgia Pacific was approached, Hines reported that the manager's first question raised the issue of unfavorable publicity that might come from animal rights groups protesting alligator hunting.

For people like the Knights who do not have the resources enjoyed by international safari hunters and multinational corporations, other factors influence both their willingness and ability to participate. The Knights paid for their lease with 35% of the value of their take. Had they been less experienced and less successful, or had hide prices fallen below a threshold value, neither the Knights nor the company would have had incentive to stay in the program.

Wild alligator hide prices have varied from a high of $58.04 per foot in 1990 to a low of $16 in 1997. Meat prices have remained fairly stable, with an average of $4.85 per pound between 1997 and 2001. In any case, the bottom line for success of the PLAMP will be determinations by private landowners to protect alligator habitat. The growth of the program throughout the early 1990s, in terms of the number of properties and total wetland acreage, suggests that the value alligators have added to wetlands may be paying off. It is also possible, and some might say likely, that some of the wetland areas incorporated into the program would not have been drained anyway, and that companies have merely continued to obey the corporate demand for profit by making money from alligator harvests. The high costs of drainage, conversion, and mitigation, in addition to the risk that the investment would be lost to periodic flooding, could have already led some owners to decide against drainage. With relaxed definitions and rules concerning **wetland mitigation,** it remains to be seen if leases for alligator harvests will be sufficient to protect wetlands.

The second criterion for evaluation involves the development of a constituency that will protect alligator habitat. If VAC is to have an impact here, user groups will need to be developed and motivated to profit the company from alligator harvests or eggs and hatchling collections, and meat and hide values must also be high enough to promote hunter effort and success. In the multibillion-dollar world of large corporations, the financial benefits discussed earlier seem insignificant. For smaller landowners and in marginal cases, opportunities to profit from wetlands might influence land-use decisions. Presumably larger properties will qualify for larger quotas. But probably of greater significance is the public relations benefit that comes from a company's being seen as "green" or "environmentally friendly"; this benefit from wetland protection could be coupled with profits from hunting leases.

Alligator Farming

"Some [farmers] have a lot more money than they have good sense," said Terry Hines. I visited Gator Gardens, an alligator farm whose manager had gone to Shellcracker Haven to hire an experienced skinner and butcher as well as young boys to scrape his hides. The manager and the owner were brothers caught up in fantasies of Wild West masculinity, roping gators instead of steers, and seeking the wealth and luxury they believed alligator farming would provide. I was reminded of pirates chasing treasure, and, it turns out, I was not far wrong. After a combination of charges for poaching eggs and hatchlings in the wild, laundering **paper alligators,** and one brother's assault on the other, the farm closed up its operations. The AMP coordinator saw it this way:

> You know there's always loopholes, and there's always bad apples. And the bad apples are going to spot the loopholes and try to finagle around them. So you're constantly trying to close loopholes. It's the same with any regulatory agency no matter what you're trying to control.

The FWC coordinator and one of the agency's biologists assured me that Gator Gardens' illegal activity was not typical of Florida alligator farm operations. Yet, through my experiences with that business, I did learn a good bit about alligator farming. It is a risky business. Among other things, it requires knowledge of program regulations and the law, an understanding of good business practices and marketing, the ability to handle large carnivores, a lot of money, and patience. Florida's active farms produced an average of over 29,000 skins and over 1.7 million pounds of meat each year between 1992 and 2001. These harvests translated into an annual average of $2.8 million in skins and just under $800,000 in meat. The number of licensed farms grew from 56 to 63 during this time, yet the number of active farms declined from 32 in 1992 to 21 in 2001 (FWC 2002a).

Alligator farmers can breed their own livestock and gather eggs and hatchlings from the wild. Operations that rely only on wild supplies have been termed "feed-lots." Breeder operations have had some difficulties: Females have been reluctant to nest where conditions were not ideal; hatch rates have been poor on occasion. These problems have made the wild supply crucial to farm survival, but because startup costs are so high, the FWC has limited the number of farms permitted for wild collection to thirty. The rationale for this decision was explained by the program coordinator:

> The idea was that you had to invest a half a million dollars or so in a facility to grow animals out and you needed to know you were going to have raw materials to put into that facility once you invested money in it. And that's a pretty difficult thing to sell, and there's critics on both sides that we need more protection for those people and others who want access to that resource. "You need to make it thirty-five . . . because I want to play."
>
> Philosophically . . . everyone should have equal access, equitable opportunity to partic-ipate. In the case of the capital investment in ranching facilities, I think it is legitimate to restrict access so as not to continue to cut the pie into smaller and smaller pieces to the detriment of the person that built the first facility to house 1/30 of the expected production.

Gator Gardens' owner claimed to have invested a million dollars in his farm, money that came from his father-in-law's multimillion-dollar hotel business in the Caribbean. The farm was an elaborate womb-to-tomb facility, incorporating breed-ing ponds, a building for incubation and hatchling nursery, two long barrackslike buildings where juveniles grew to their slaughter size of six feet, a "kill-pen," and a processing building. Here alligators became "a smoked product" for which the farm received between $12 and $15 per pound, jars of dip, boxes of cubed fillets, empty skins, and disembodied heads and feet.

The manager took me first to visit the nursery. The temperature- and humidity-controlled house contained thirty-six fiberglass tubs of about 18 cubic feet each,

Jane W. Gibson

Gator Gardens, an industrial alligator farm

stacked in three layers. Nine held elongated, leathery eggs packed in sphagnum moss. Incubation temperature determines the sex of alligators, so thermostats were set to produce faster-growing, potentially bigger males. New hatchlings swam and floated in the other tubs that they shared with baby turtles.

The first barracks we entered held older alligator babies in concrete pools that ran down both walls of the building. These pools, separated by masonry walls and an elevated sidewalk between the two rows, measured about 80 square feet, and each contained about thirty small alligators. Fiberglass containers identical to those of the nursery hung suspended above the pools. These contained the newest hatchlings from the nursery.

The second barracks contained alligators nearing 6 feet long, the size the owner and manager had determined would be optimum for harvest. Alligators first enter the pool at one end, and as they grow, work their way around the room and back to the door. As males grow older, they become more aggressive, especially as they approach an age for mating. Fighting damages their valuable hides, so owners take care not to crowd their "investment" in the final months before slaughter. I was not surprised to learn that harvest size would be related to hide prices. When these dropped from their high of $38 per foot in 1990 to $13 per foot in 1993, farmers slaughtered sooner to reduce rearing costs. The average harvest length between 1992 and 2001 was less than 5 feet.

After leaving the alligator houses, we walked down a path cut between native grasses and trees to the breeding ponds, canals that were carved out of the land. According to their official report, they had 125 male and female adults that produced only 15 nests with 727 eggs of which only 215, less than one third, hatched. These farmers did not know when they built their ponds that female alligators are solitary nesters; the ponds did not provide sufficient privacy.

Alligators at Gator Gardens eat poultry by-products that give even recently cleaned pens a putrid smell. Some farms use the by-products of commercial fisheries or slaughterhouses. On this diet, and in the temperature-controlled environment, alligators never stop growing. Growth that would ordinarily take about six years in the wild can be reduced to two and a half to three years on an alligator farm. Another advantage of captive rearing is better hide quality because accelerated growth reduces the time spent in the company of other alligators that bite in competition for food and mates.

When Gator Gardens' alligators reached 6 feet, as measured along the masonry blocks of the wall, they were removed with a kind of snare attached to the end of a pole. I watched as an employee dragged an alligator to the outdoor kill-pen. Here the alligator joined a dozen others behind the chain-link fence. These alligators would wait for several days without food because, otherwise, "they tend to get a little messy on the table." Farmers use different methods of slaughter. Some use guns or **bang sticks.** The manager at Gator Gardens preferred an axe whose blade he buried behind the alligator's skull to sever its spinal cord. The dead animals would then be hung from a meat hook in a cooler before processing, using methods identical to those used in Shellcracker Haven's skinning shed.

Gator Gardens contracted with a tannery I visited in Tarpon Springs to turn "green skins" into highly polished, tanned leather. These they sold to buyers in New York for the most part. They sold their smoked alligator fillets to Florida theme parks such as Disneyworld. Millions from around the world can now consume "gatorburgers," which are offered on the menu of Disney's corporate American fantasies of free markets and social and ecological harmony.

The Public Hunt

No one in Shellcracker Haven has the resources to build and run an alligator farm. Instead, their main entry into the opportunities provided by the AMP is in the lottery-based public hunt. But this was not always the case.

The GFC initiated experimental hunts in 1981 as part of a study designed to determine the sustainable harvest of alligators. The agency relied on Shellcracker Haven's experienced trappers whose participation depended in part on how close they lived to the habitat they would hunt. Fourteen men from Shellcracker Haven, including Mr. Knight's grandson, received permits for the experimental hunt in 1987. They came from four households in the community that year, compared to ten the year before. Together, they made up 50% of the hunters in 1986 and 70% in 1987. The GFC paid for these experiments by taking 30% of hide values, but this still left between $5,000 and $5,500 for each family, a significant contribution to household incomes. The GFC determined that each participating hunter averaged a benefit of $5,029 per year between 1981 and 1987, the years in which experimental hunts took place.

Alligator hunts on Shellcracker Basin lakes remained tightly controlled until 1988, the year the GFC opened up the hunt to the public by implementing a selection process based on the use of a lottery. In the first year, 5,855 applicants vied for 238 permits. The pool jumped to more than 20,000 in the second year, severely reducing the odds that Shellcracker Haven hunters might be selected. And whereas hunters could take fifteen alligators each in the early years of the public hunts, today they can only take two. The reduction in the number of alligators each licensed hunter can take has allowed the agency to include more applicants, each of whom pays $250 for a license ($1,000 if the hunter is from out-of-state), plus $20 for each of the two CITES tags to be affixed to harvested alligators. In the 2001 public hunt, 7,871 hunters threw their names in the hat for 1,533 permits. These program rule changes distributed access to alligators to many more hunters, reduced the odds that traditional trappers would be selected, reduced the economic benefits of participation, and increased revenue to the agency by about $324,000.

Another important change related to the hunters themselves. From the earlier requirements for participation, including residence and experience, the new method invited a very different group. The AMP managers collected demographic data on hunters for the first time in 1990. Over 90% of respondents identified as "white," three respondents identified as American Indian, and ten as Hispanic. Their incomes varied widely. Nearly 17% said they earned $0 to $15,000; 27% earned $15,001 to $25,000; 34% earned $25,001 to $50,000; and 22% earned more than $50,000 per year. Thirteen percent did not complete high school; 40% had a high school diploma only; and 48% had some college education. In this last group, six had earned graduate degrees. The new hunter group was better educated and had higher incomes, but they did not necessarily have the experience and knowledge of Shellcracker Haven's trappers, nor were they tied to the lakes of the region through family histories.

Clouds diffused the setting sunlight early one September evening while winds ruffled the tea-colored waters of the lake. We could smell the approaching storm that would limit the night's take. Still hunters from all over the state came with their airboats and small fishing boats from which they would hunt the ancient reptiles. Under the watchful eyes of armed wildlife officers, they would "put in," that is, launch their boats from the concrete ramp. Then at 7:17 P.M., the time designated for the gator hunt to begin, they would leave the protection of the cove and head into weedy, alligator territories.

Waters at the lake edge began to fill as one driver after another backed trailers down the ramp to launch their boats. Next to the fishing boats, airboats loomed large, with giant propellers, jet engines, and sometimes elaborately painted tail fins. An especially impressive boat bore a skull and crossbones with fire-lit eyes and a snake-entwined sword thrust through its cranium. Another was painted in camouflage colors that matched many hunters' hats, shirts, and jackets. This ruse that might have hidden trappers against a forest background would do little good on the lake in the dark. Under these conditions, alligators identify their predators by the sounds of engines and the smells of fuel, insect repellant, and humans.

Standing on the bank, the Knights identified one man as a novice. His tidy button-down shirt, tucked neatly into pleated khaki pants, would have drawn no attention were he smoking his expensive cigar while seated behind a desk. Instead he stood beside a small boat, preparing to hunt a large, reptilian carnivore that sits at the top of its food chain. The Knights expressed no small amount of consternation at this man's inexperienced, recreational use of resources on which the Knights and others depended for their livelihoods. Mr. Knight had strong feelings about this matter:

> They give people permits from Miami to hunt Shellcracker Basin lakes, which is ridiculous. A man comes all the way from Miami to these lakes. Never seen one or know anything about it. That's ridiculous.

Jane W. Gibson

A trapper helps guide the trailer carrying his airboat as it backs toward the lake edge. Soon he and his son will take off across the lake to hunt alligators.

Not all newcomers to alligator hunting were so conspicuous. Two gray-haired beginners blended perfectly with veteran hunters in their ball caps and t-shirts. My conversation with them revealed their inexperience as well as their motives.

First hunter: We never hunted nothing in our lives. Not even sparrows.

Second hunter: I went deer hunting one time and seen a little baby deer and said, aw, I can't shoot that. To hell with it. I'm going home.

Third hunter: Them sparrows are dangerous, ain't they B?

First hunter: You better believe it!

JG: Why did you decide to do this now? Isn't it a little dangerous?

First hunter: That's why! Just the challenge. We've done a little bit of everything but this, and we're gonna try this. This might be our first and last time tonight. [laughs]

Second hunter: We've tried airplanes. We've tried racecars. We've tried racing boats. Now we're gonna try this.

Experienced hunters, especially those who had made part of their living from gator hides in the past, shared the newcomers' appreciation for the excitement of hunting a large carnivore, but they added personal experience to their stories.

JG: So you're a practiced gator hunter?

First trapper: Well, I wouldn't consider myself that, but I fooled with them in the late '50s and early '60s before they shut [legal hunting] down. . . . They shut it down in '62. I hunted up until then. I have gators on my property. I haven't killed any in years, but I fool with them all the time. They're right there on my property.

JG: Can you call up a gator?

First trapper: There's two sounds you make. There's the mating call, and the sound the young make when you're molesting them, a squeaky sound [makes the sound]. When they squeak, look out! There comes a big one!

JG: So you think people might get hurt?

First trapper: There's always that possibility, but everybody out here's grown. More or less, they should be.

First hunter: [laughs] They will be when they get back!

JG: [as another experienced trapper joins the conversation] Are you a professional hunter?

Second trapper: [grins] Well, no, not legally anyhow. [laughter]

JG: What's the size limit this evening?

Second trapper: Anything over 4 feet. You get anything under 4 feet, you've got to eat it right there on the spot.

The hunters continued their conversations while checking equipment and supplies. Two fishers cast lines into the lake from a pier, now elevated well above the water after many months of drought. A crowd of observers gathered on the bank. No animal rights defenders appeared among them that evening, though the GFC was prepared for them. Only families with children, journalists, students, hunters not drawn in the lottery, I with Dave, a videographer, and other curious people watched the gathering of hunters and boats. The GFC's wildlife officers arrived in officially marked, green trucks pulling green boats with police lights, and bearing the official state agency seal. Their uniforms bore insignia of rank, badges, and agency patches. The law grants them full police powers, and they wore their sidearms to oversee the hunt.

Man: They don't let me hunt anymore. Got me for poaching. Several times.

Woman: Here they come now. I'm telling you.

Man: The Big Man.

Excitement grew as the time to begin the hunt drew near. As though to release some of the tension, hunters started boat engines, revved them like dragsters at the starting line, shot out of the cove a hundred yards, turned, and roared back to shore. The sun posed orange, low in the purple sky. Wind began to gust, bringing the expected storm, and rain fell. The lake turned dark and choppy. At last, officers began the check for hunting licenses and properly equipped boats. They provided new information and answered questions: "Gators have to be killed upon capture." "Be sure to put a numbered tag on them." "You can use a bang stick, harpoon, or snatch hook." "Hides must be skinned according to these specifications."

Finally, it was time to go. Boats roared to life again, this time slowly moving away from shore and into the places where the alligators had begun their own night-time hunt. Dave and I got a ride with the sergeant who would be cruising the lake until 1 A.M., when everyone had to be back onshore. Our boat seemed to bounce across the waves, past floating mats made of water lilies, hyacinths, and hydrilla. Within minutes, the sun disappeared, rain fell harder, and lights from distant boats danced in all directions as hunters scanned for prey.

We "shined" two alligator yearlings, eyes reflecting opaque gold disks from where they floated. Each was no more than a foot of striped and speckled shiny black

Jane W. Gibson

The GFC arrived in force.

scales. They swam away from our light, using their tails to propel themselves into the water lilies where glossy, green leaves the size of dinner plates shielded them from hungry, adult males, and from us. With our motor now off, we could hear sounds of the other boats and excited voices carrying across the water. We spotted a boat that was stopped cold, its light fixed on a spot at the edge of an aquatic weed mat. The hunters in the boat were about to take their first gator.

We pulled in closer to see that the boat was already alongside the alligator. The experienced hunter had secured the animal with a gig inserted by harpoon at a place high on the animal's back. The gator jerked when it felt the jab, causing the gig to rotate under the skin, securing its death with the link between alligator and man. The hunter carefully positioned his bang stick to fire the cartridge into the base of the alligator's skull. Sparks flew over the splash of the thrashing animal, and we heard the explosion as the sound of the bang stick reached our ears.

We pulled up closer still and watched as the hunters looped a rope around the gator's head and, together, pulled the heavy corpse up onto the boat. The sergeant studied the length along the gator's snout between nose and eyes and estimated that it was probably 6 feet long, well above the legal minimum. "Nice shot!" the hunters congratulated each other. They tagged their catch, complained that the weather was making hunting difficult, and relived the excitement of the kill. "He's a nice gator."

Alligator program biologists met successful hunters as they returned to shore. The scientists recorded tag numbers and weighed, sexed, and measured every animal killed, so the crowd of observers, now grown significantly, shared in one final spectacle of the hunt. Hunters then loaded gators onto trucks to be taken quickly to coolers, where they would remain until processors could skin and butcher them.

The FWC continues to classify the public hunt as a commercial venture because the hides and meat have market value. Yet a survey of participants in the 1989 hunt

Jane W. Gibson

A nice gator

administered in January of 1990, with a response rate of 63%, showed that only 2 of the 139 hunters who returned the completed questionnaire (of the 222 participating permit holders) relied on commercial fishing or trapping for even half of their annual household income. These two, representing a little over 1% of respondents, said they depended on these activities for between 75 and 100% of their livelihood. Most (69% in 1988 and 77% in 1989) had no experience hunting alligators at all, and over 83% said they derived no income from hunting and fishing. Nevertheless, money does appear on the list of motivations identified by 75% in 1988 and 50% in 1989. Of these, however, only 9% and 7% respectively identified money as their sole incentive for participation. Other reasons given included for sport, for a trophy, and application for the purpose of improving someone else's chances of participation.

In 1990, after a rule change that required that license holders be in the boat during the hunt, the number of applicants for hunting licenses dropped by half. In the new, more inclusive lottery, the economic incentive is also reduced. Following the theory of value-added conservation, it would follow logically that reduced income means reduced interest in the health of alligator populations. This cost would, in turn, reduce the likelihood that the program will generate an effective constituency ready to act to prevent the habitat degradation and destruction that threaten alligator populations. And, because income from hunting is reduced, income to families in Shellcracker Haven is also reduced. We must consider the consequences of that for the long run. It may be that the longevity of alligators and Shellcracker Haven in particular, and biological and cultural diversity in general, may depend on noneconomic values to bolster their defenses. And it may be that linking biological and cultural diversity offers the best hope for the preservation of both. It is to these issues that we now turn.

5/Can We Conserve
Wild Species
and Communities?

Today, I cannot buy a wild catfish fillet at my neighborhood market because almost all catfish sold today are raised on farms. In 1989, catfishers in Shellcracker Haven received 80 cents per pound from the local wholesaler who sold the fish to a dealer for 90 cents per pound. Restaurants in the area would pay as much as $4 per pound, but their demand was very small and each had an established relationship with a fisherman. The little money families received for their efforts rewarded the wife or daughter, who fed some 700 hooks on about 2,100 feet of line into fish boxes. It rewarded the labor required to bait these hooks, the hour and a half to set the lines, three hours to pull catfish from the lake, and more hours, depending on the day's catch, to clean them. Catfish income contributed to boat and truck maintenance, gasoline, fishing gear, and freezer maintenance; and it helped feed, clothe, and house the fisherman's family. In the fifteen catfishing families I knew, there was never enough to cover higher education and health insurance.

The fisher's and trapper's successes are understood to be significantly economic, but not only that. Success brings personal esteem and family pride, and in kin-based communities like Shellcracker Haven, with a fishing and hunting tradition that dates back over a hundred years, these activities link families to the past as they reenact the work and social life of parents and grandparents. In short, fishing and hunting are the centerpiece of a collective identity that is rooted in shared memories, experiences, kinship, and worldview and is marked and reinforced by behavior and affection.

RETHINKING VALUE

In the Alligator Management Program (AMP), the FWC (Florida Fish and Wildlife Conservation Commission) pinned its hope for conservation on effective law enforcement and value-added conservation (VAC). "Value" in this case is explicitly economic, and it is theorized to vest hunters in the well-being of alligators and their habitats. We know that being able to make money from an alligator hide and its meat does add to the set of motivations that bring sports and commercial trappers to the

Jane W. Gibson

Before the drought, water lapped the bottom of the dock and sometimes flowed over it. Here, determined fishers pole their boats through muck and aquatic weeds to deeper water.

hunt. And given the higher average incomes of sport hunters, the economic benefit to traditional trappers' families likely means more to this group when measured as a percentage of annual income.

But while money is an especially important incentive for the families of Shellcracker Haven to fish and to hunt alligators, sports enthusiasts and traditional fishers and trappers alike appreciate the challenge and excitement of pulling in a large, feisty fish and hunting and killing large, exotic carnivores.

I asked Mr. Knight about his experience of hunting alligators: "Tell me what it's like. How do you go about it?"

Never a man to "talk your ear off," he paused and answered, "You just see his eye, go to him, and try to get him. That's about all you can do."

I waited for more to follow this efficient answer, but when no other comments came, I finally asked, "Do you enjoy it?"

At once, Mr. Knight became animated. He leaned forward in the cypress swing, his eyes sparkling, and his smile wide. "Yeah! I *love* it, you know!" Then he leaned back abruptly, punctuating the profundity of his testimonial.

Why do such statements matter? The people of Shellcracker Haven value the financial gain to be had from selling hides and meat. In fact, they need it. But they also value other things: They value a way of life and a tradition that go back several generations, and they value their autonomy. When Owens-Illinois proposed to build condominiums on the lake, this proposal did not just threaten the health of the alligator population, but also threatened a way of life. The condos would bring newcomers, nonkin who would affect the relations and dynamics of the kin-based town. They would bring with them traffic, noise, and outsider behaviors and pejorative views of local families and their lives on Shellcracker Lake. And, as they have done

Late one night, some unidentified residents took out their frustrations with "the authorities" and "repaired" the dam's notch with concrete.

in new neighborhood developments to the north, they would influence policies regarding the lake, and not necessarily in ways with which experienced, long-term residents would agree.

Such was the case when drought combined with hydrilla, an aquatic weed that clogged water-cooled boat motors, to undermine lake-based businesses. Retirees living north of Red's Fish Camp, Red himself, and other marina owners found their boats sitting in mud and their fish camps and marinas in trouble.

They appealed for help. Some wanted the areas around their docks dredged so they would refill with water and allow boaters to get out onto the lake. Some wanted to see sterile carp introduced to feed on the hydrilla. (Because this group had ties to a state legislator, alarms went off. Sterile carp are not always sterile, according to fisheries biologists, and their voracious appetites can eliminate all aquatic vegetation and, as a result, the fishery!) Another group thought the low-water dam, built years ago when lake levels fell, was the cause of the present problem. A notch had been cut out of it, allowing water to flow through the opening when the lake was high. Closing the notch was this group's solution.

In several public meetings, aquatic weed specialists, fisheries biologists, and representatives from the Army Corps of Engineers pointed out to residents and business owners that dredging would afford a short-term solution only. Carp would turn the fishing lake into a skiing lake, and the dam was irrelevant because lake levels had fallen so low that the only thing the dam held back was mud. The views of these specialists matched those of the few who attended from Shellcracker Haven. The community members' long history on the lake had taught them that lakes rise and fall and then rise again, and that this natural process is normal and good for the freshwater species that live there. Not only do residents of Shellcracker Haven understand lake

Jane W. Gibson

The state sprayed the lake with an expensive aquatic herbicide to "knock back" the hydrilla, when drought undermined lake-based businesses.

hydrology and its relationship to fish and alligators, but they also know that new-comers to the lake do not understand these relationships. In light of their experience, knowledge, and willingness to stand up against destructive proposals, support for their livelihood strategies might well become a state priority.

Participation in the experimental hunts added significantly to the extended family's income and enthusiasm before implementation of the statewide lottery system in 1988. That year, no one from the family was selected to receive a hunting permit, but the men found inexperienced hunters and signed on as their agents. The next year, two Knights were drawn in the lottery, and the family contracted to process an additional two permits, which at that time meant a potential total of 60 alligators plus any nuisance gators Mr. Knight brought in. The total for the month was about 90 alligators processed over a period of 20 days. This was a good season for the family. Mr. Knight's grandson played happily in the skinning shed, making engine noises for his toy airboat. Two blue-eyed blonde babies entertained themselves in a playpen in the corner.

Throughout the month, the family's social-ecological world received fortification. Everyone worked hard to process the stream of alligators Mr. Knight and his son carried from the cooler to the skinning shed. They told stories about the hunt and about their children and grandchildren, shared information, sought advice from each other, entertained visitors to the skinning shed, and planned for the future.

We can probably agree with Robinson and Redford (1991) that if wildlife has no use to people, it will be assigned no value either; and if it has no value, it can be allowed to disappear. And while it follows that when people use wildlife, wildlife will have value, it does not follow that the associated value will be at all economic, let alone exclusively so. Nor does it follow, as the theory of VAC supposes, that because wildlife takes on economic value when it enters the marketplace, policies for its conservation should be considered only in economic terms.

Herbert Schroeder, an environmental psychologist, notes the importance of the different kinds of experiences people have in natural environments. He sees expressions of value in the ways people talk about their experiences and identifies these values as keys to successful natural resource management. He writes that *emotion* and *motivation* share a common root that means "to move." *Value* comes from the Latin *valere,* meaning to be strong. To say that something has value is to say that it has the power to move us—to arouse our emotions and motivate or push us into action. Schroeder argues that "value and emotion are inseparable" (Schroeder 1996:18–19). Thus he laments that science, charged with providing sound biological data aimed at species and habitat protection, does not see the emotion, attitudes, perceptions, imagination, and intuition of the human experience in nature as valid and important because they are subjective phenomena and difficult to measure.

Emotional attachment to the lakes and forests of Shellcracker Basin is the value that most clearly distinguishes the community's hunters and fishers from those sports enthusiasts with whom they share an economic interest and excitement for the challenge of going up against other species, particularly large, carnivorous ones. Remember that Mr. Knight used the word *love* to describe his experience of hunting and that it was he and his kin, not sports enthusiasts, whose affective ties motivated them to stand against a powerful corporation. But because such nonquantifiable values do not lend themselves to scientific measurement, they do not figure into natural resource management models.

In fact, social factors, though known to be important in effective management and increasingly incorporated in developing countries, tend to be marginalized in U.S. natural resource management, if they are included at all. One important reason for this is that rural communities, whose voices might be incorporated into management decisions, tend to be poor and less well-educated, at least insofar as formal educational institutions are concerned. The result is that local knowledge and skills such communities have to offer are denied authority because they bear neither scientific credentials nor the markers of economic rationality, both central to modern natural resource management (Lockie, Higgins, and Lawrence, 2001). Furthermore, the view that people and other species occupy separate spheres works against traditional hunters and fishers. As the coordinator of the AMP put it, "Those people are really not my concern." On the contrary, the continued decline of Florida's biodiversity suggests that they ought to be.

ENDANGERED EXPERIENCES

The strength of personal attachments to the land and lakes of Shellcracker Basin has been sorely tested and raises questions about the community's longevity. Their lifeways, experiences, and ties to Shellcracker Basin might be thought of as a specialized set of "endangered experiences" that are linked to natural environments (Schroeder 1996).

National economic restructuring in the naval stores industry and agriculture has eliminated these livelihood strategies in the community, and over a half-century of natural resource management has eroded traditional access to and use of wild species. There was a time when families produced their subsistence without the

Jane W. Gibson

Today, the railroad transports Florida's forests.

mediation of middlemen and an export market, and without the intervention of professional fish and wildlife managers. Vegetables planted with human muscle and horse- or mule-drawn plows moved from field to pantry, often by way of the canner. Wild and domestic animals went to the smokehouse or the cookstove. Fish went from the fisherman's seine or line to the fish house for processing and to the stewpot. Community identities as farmers and fishers were firmly rooted in the land and Shellcracker Lake through tradition and necessity.

The same railroad that brought newcomers made market participation outside the community a reality, and recreational hunting and fishing an opportunity for the state that would require fish and wildlife management. The heated battle between recreational and commercial fishers, with natural resource managers in the middle, ended with the stroke of a pen in the state capitol, and Shellcracker Haven lost its mainstay.

The FWC grew in size and strength from its relationship with sport hunters and fishers, now blending science, politics, enforcement, and public relations to retain support from recreational users for the agency's constitutional authority. The price for that support was Jack Dequine's job, the livelihood of freshwater commercial fishers (a group that included half the families in Shellcracker Haven), a loosening of the bond between freshwater fishers and the fishery habitats on which they depend, and a fish and wildlife management agency captured by the singular, but powerful recreational constituency.

Production in Shellcracker Haven has always been limited by the labor available in families, simple technologies, and small, local markets. These conditions have ensured that harvests of wild species are kept at sustainable levels. But poverty and long-term erosion of community access and use of species have threatened the way of life for the people of Shellcracker Haven, and those affective attachments that have led them to defend Shellcracker Basin.

Poverty comes with painful consequences. Some may be inclined to adopt high-risk behaviors that draw attention from unwelcome outsiders such as social workers or the county sheriff. Inability to afford dental care, healthy diets, and medical insurance can leave physical markers of their financial disadvantages. Locals know how they are perceived outside their community and react against stereotyped characterizations of poor whites.

Yet, the older generation in Shellcracker Haven, who would like to have earned more money, make statements that affirm the higher value they place on the security of family and community support. As Mrs. Knight said, "I wouldn't be nowheres else but here." The younger generation, however, may not share their parents' and grandparents' views. **Consumerism** may to be winning the hearts and minds of youth.

Consumerism describes a key component of America's free market ideology. President George W. Bush recently told Americans to shop as an expression of patriotism, since it is consumption that drives the nation's flagging economy. Through ubiquitous advertising, consumerism encourages us to prefer new things to used ones, to buy them now on readily available credit cards instead of later with cash, and to work more to pay off our mounting consumer debt. We have learned to reckon social status through display of the things we own, to imagine and reinvent ourselves through the experiences of consumption, and to form attachments to things that compete with attachments to people. And as things ultimately fail to fill the emotional gaps created by the erosion of our social and emotional relations with people, we consume more to stave off the loneliness. What this analysis suggests is not only that the close social networks found among the poor arise and are maintained out of necessity, but that poverty protects against consumerism that has yet to drive its wedges fully into social relations. This is not to say, however, that mechanisms for dissemination of consumerist values are not hard at work among the poor.

As described in Chapter 1, Shellcracker Haven is rural and remote, yet satellite dishes decorate yards and channel images of affluence into local living rooms. The demand for things has been on the rise in the community—most conspicuously among its children.

Jimmy came often to visit my daughters when we lived in Shellcracker Haven. He was already a little weathered at the young age of 13; he had been toughened by hard work. In fact, Jimmy missed a lot of school so he could stay home and help his father in the newest business in the community, the sale of braided sticks to the artificial plant industry. The money Jimmy earned went for brand-name shoes, jeans, shirts, and sunglasses. Like most boys his age, he had his eye on girls and "cool stuff." An education might have helped him in the long-run to earn more than his dad, a commercial fisherman in addition to his new stick business, but Jimmy made "good money," by a child's standards if he stayed home from school to work with his dad.

Mr. Knight's grown son, Jimmy's cousin, quit high school when he came to the same conclusion. He once explained to me, "I went to that school, and they didn't teach me nothing I needed to know about airboats or hunting, so I came home." But I heard this son and his wife encouraging their own sons in their schoolwork despite the younger Mr. Knight's earlier assessment of public schools. I believe they realized that children with some credentials could expect to earn more than high school dropouts could hope to. Yet these children will have to leave the security of kin and community for higher incomes elsewhere. Or they may find ways to earn more close

Children work, even at the expense of their education, to be able to buy "cool stuff."

to home, perhaps by intensifying production based on the extraction of raw materials and wildlife in Shellcracker Basin. Or we could propose a third alternative: Just as the agency currently protects the interests of alligator farmers because their financial investment is high, they could protect the interests of rural communities because their investments run deep.

LOCAL MANAGERS

There is growing acceptance that top-down management models fail because they ignore or pay too little attention to local priorities (Jeffery and Vira 2001). Furthermore, as the public becomes increasingly aware of natural resource issues, there is greater reluctance to accept unquestioningly the authority of professionals (Ewert 1996).

It might be tempting to see the decline of Florida's biodiversity as failure of the FWC and reason enough to return management of fragile ecosystems to those who love and depend on them. But arguments that local input is necessary must also recognize that, even if local knowledge were sufficient in the past, it is unlikely to be sufficient under current conditions, which include pressures on local producers to increase their harvests, a fact that should temper any tendencies we might have to romanticize producers.

Consider frog hunting in Shellcracker Haven, as it is revealed through Bull's story. Bull wears a helmet with a light attached to the front and places a four-pronged spear and a sack on his airboat. It is nearly 10 P.M., there is a sliver of moon in the cloudless sky, and Bull is going frog gigging. Around the shallow edges of Shellcracker Lake, only the shrill screech of cicadas competes with the rhythmic chanting of frogs: high-pitched trills mixed with the deep, throaty sound of bullfrogs,

Bull's preferred prey. He cuts the engine on his airboat, and soon the music rises as he shines his light across water hyacinths and lily pads where reflective frog eyes and white chins reveal their hiding places. The light shone in a frog's eyes holds it on the surface, like a deer "caught" in the headlights of a car. Bull silently poles his boat to within gigging range, moves the spear into position behind the frog, and strikes through the soft body. He removes the still-kicking frog and places it in the sack. When the sack is full or Bull has run out of steam, he goes home where the night's catch will be refrigerated. The next morning, he and his wife, Naomi, will remove and skin the legs for sale to a local restaurant.

Bull began frogging in 1962 when, on an especially successful night, he shared the lake with many other hunters and could still produce 100 pounds of frog legs by himself. The day I met him and Naomi in their skinning shed, they had only a few small packages from the recent harvest. Bull explained that overhunting has contributed to the dramatic decline in frog populations in Shellcracker Basin that has left him as the sole practitioner in the community today. In the early 1980s, he said, his take had fallen to an average 45 to 50 pounds each night, and by 1989, when he still counted as many as 20 other hunters on the lake, his average had fallen to 25 pounds.

Other factors reduced Bull's take, beginning with aquatic weed infestations. Bull explained that even though Florida hunters may gig year-round, frogs are difficult to spot except in winter when the weeds die back. He also pointed out that there are fewer frogs because the drought dried up critical marshy habitat where the frog population reproduced.

Though Bull continues late-night frog gigging, he admits that he can hardly make enough money to pay for the gasoline used in hauling and operating his 150-horse-power airboat. Another frogger estimated the cost in 1990 of operating an airboat for a night at between $20 and $25 and said he would have to take 10 to 12 pounds to break even. Bull reported that prices paid for frog legs in 1990 were sometimes as low as $1.50 per pound, half of what they were in 1989, and his last effort netted only 5 pounds. Because the frogs he finds now are few and small compared to those of just a few years ago, and because fuel prices have risen while frog prices have dropped, the future of Bull's primary business is in serious doubt. Clearly the health of the frog population is also at risk as froggers continue to hunt them.

Where local knowledge and emotional attachments to ecosystems born of shared memories and traditional uses have produced sustainable exploitation, user populations have been small, their technologies simple, and rules for access exclusive of outsiders. Even though sometimes what is produced and sold winds up in international markets, these systems also tend toward production for subsistence and local markets. Such common property systems are rare, but not unknown in market economies. In the United States, the drive to make a profit, and constant inflationary pressure on the costs of living and doing business, compel extractors to adopt more complex, labor-saving technologies to increase production for sale, even beyond the ability of species to recover from overexploitation. Or they drive producers out altogether.

Bull's experience with frogging on Shellcracker Lake has the potential to become Garrett Hardin's "tragedy" (Hardin 1968). In Hardin's tale, each farmer enjoys the full benefit of every cow he feeds from a shared grassland while the cost to the grassland is distributed across the total number of farmers. At some point, since farmers do not experience the full cost of adding more cows, the herds exceed the **carrying**

capacity of the pastures and the grassland collapses, presumably taking the cattle and the farmers' livelihood with it. Missing from Hardin's open-access pasture and Shellcracker Lake for froggers are the institutionalized rules concerning access. Anyone with cows could graze them on the shared pasture; anyone with a **gig** and insect repellent can hunt frogs on Shellcracker Lake.

Incorporation of traditional users into management programs will be necessary to fortify rural communities whose members' affective ties may lead them to protect healthy ecosystems and biodiversity. But their contributions alone will not be sufficient. External conditions within which members of rural communities exist and relate have to be changed.

BEYOND THE LOCAL

Exclusive management of fish and wildlife by small-scale commercial users would be most severely limited by forces far beyond the local context. Florida's population growth averages just under 700 people per day. In a study of the causes of Florida's problem of urban sprawl, Kolankiewicz and Beck (2001) found that between 1950 and 2000, the state's population grew from 2.8 million to 16 million and is projected to reach 20.7 million by 2025. New arrivals have fueled the profitability of development while simultaneously explaining 85% of sprawl. In the two decades examined for their study (1970–1990), residents spread out over an additional one million acres, bringing conversion of natural habitats to a full 40% of the state.

To reiterate a bottom-line measure of FWC success cited earlier, 261 of 532 (49.1%) terrestrial species and 46 of 126 (29.1%) freshwater fish species are suspected or known to be in decline in Florida (OPPAGA 2001:7–12). Kolankiewicz and Beck (2001) found the damage to be even greater. More than 600 species in South Florida are considered rare or imperiled, and the federal government has listed 68 species as threatened or endangered. We humans continue to colonize the wilderness, drain wetlands, cut forests, spray pesticides, apply fertilizers, and pour concrete, causing fish and wildlife to sicken with poisons and their habitats to shrink with development.

That these losses result from forces beyond the scope of FWC authority in no way diminishes the fact that the agency is doomed to fail in its conservation mission unless these trends can be halted. At a minimum, ways to limit population growth in the state will need to be addressed, as will the need to curtail development. A constitutional change will also be necessary to bring an end to assaults on air and water related to wild species habitats under agency authority. Floridians identify sprawl as a major concern because of consequences for biodiversity (Kolankiewicz and Beck 2001), but little in the popular press or elsewhere has helped them to link the problem to its causes. Thus, education will be necessary to shine a light on this relationship and, most importantly, on the relationship between the health and viability of the state's dominant mammal, *Homo sapiens,* and the well-being of all nonvoting species.

These changes cannot be accomplished overnight, though it is clear that a sense of urgency is warranted. An alternative process of building the political movement around the constituency to which VAC aspires—an approach being tested in other parts of the world where rural ecosystems, biodiversity, and human populations have also suffered—could be applied in Florida. This approach has been termed participatory natural resource management.

Jane W. Gibson

These canals drain the surrounding wetland to create this "muck farm," which is owned by a prominent Florida family.

PARTICIPATORY NATURAL RESOURCE MANAGEMENT

Where resources are in decline, social conflict is often a significant contributing factor, sometimes because wars ensue, but also because individuals attempt to continue a way of life dependent on natural resources to which they no longer have sufficient access. Wondolleck (1991) suggests three other sources of conflict, all applicable to the Florida case. One is that a resource-user group has captured an agency through the exertion of political power. Florida's recreational hunters and fishers accomplished this feat when, in exchange for an end to commercial freshwater fishing, the Florida Wildlife Federation agreed to throw its weight behind the constitutional amendment that created the GFC (Florida Game and Fresh Water Fish Commission). We have only to remember the AMP coordinator's statement about those whose livelihoods depend on access to fisheries and wildlife—they simply are not his concern. A second source of conflict identified by Wondolleck occurs when an agency's management options have been limited by budgetary or legislative mandates. The FWC may have autonomy from legislative caprice, but its budget still comes through the legislature, paid largely by sports hunters and fishers. Third, Wondolleck notes that conflict arises when an agency deliberately ignores some groups because of real or imagined power. The agency's constitutional authority specifically excludes the causes of air and water pollution, much of which is generated by the beneficiaries of "development" and industrial agriculture.

Far from the "silver bullet" we might wish for, participation of communities associated with fragile ecosystems is nevertheless deemed necessary to turn conflict into cooperation in achieving shared management goals. It has been proposed that local people should be involved from the beginning in the design, management, monitoring, and evaluation of projects and programs instituted to reverse a history of destruction (Jeffrey and Vira 2001). We know that the notion of participation is sometimes nothing more than lip service, as in the case of passive participation when people simply do what they are told by authorities, but under the right conditions, it can be much closer to the ideal.

Elinor Ostrom (1996:1082) identified conditions under which participatory solutions can improve on top-down initiatives or solely local ones. First, resources contributed by governments and citizens must be complementary and offer opportunities for synergy. The FWC's sophistication in politics, education and outreach, and public relations will be invaluable complements to their financial resources and technical expertise in this effort. Rural communities can bring skills, intimate local knowledge, multifaceted motivation, and need.

Second, both parties must be legally entitled to make decisions, leaving them both some flexibility. This condition implies the need for shared knowledge and training of local participants, as well as the third condition: Participants need to make credible commitments to each other, perhaps through contracts, mutual trust, or by enhancing social ties. Fourth, incentives must exist to encourage the participation of all stakeholders.

Participatory projects will thus present numerous challenges in Florida. Stakeholders must all be identified with recognition that between and even within groups, there may well be different interests, unequal power, and those with greater or lesser capacity for participation. One stakeholder in Florida that might be most reluctant to participate is the FWC itself, since participation will imply relinquishing some control to people they do not necessarily know or trust. Indeed, wildlife officers are trained and positioned to interact most with those who break the law. The multitudes who do not seldom interact with the organization. It seems likely, however, that biologists and program managers will be sensitive to the inevitably increasing pressure for the agency to overcome forces that work against conservation.

Building an alliance with rural communities of commercial users of fish and wildlife, recreational users, and environmentalists will seem a prudent, albeit difficult, step. Sports hunters and fishers need to hear the message they resisted over 50 years ago when Jack Dequine's research demonstrated a symbiotic relationship between commercial and recreational fishing. This will mean giving technical, regulatory, and political support to the livelihood strategies of commercial users, even if it means, for example, that alligator trappers have first priority in the lottery and are permitted to fill larger quotas to meet their families' basic needs. Traditional users must be assured of the reliability and stability of their stakes; history has taught people in Shellcracker Haven that making ends meet is a daily challenge because what they can do today might not be available tomorrow. And because this group is the one most clearly and profoundly vested in the health of local biodiversity, professionalization that built pride and stature in the FWC and in Mr. Knight will need to be extended to many others in Shellcracker Haven and to other such communities.

Finally, environmentalists, too, should join this alliance, recognizing that the cause of Florida's environmental crisis rests largely with unrestrained population growth and unrestrained **urban sprawl.** The problem will not be solved by attacking those who value wildlife in diverse ways, some of whom must take it to make a living, but rather in standing against those who can see it only in economic terms. It is they who destroy habitat for the greater economic rewards earned from its pollution and wholesale conversion into slash pine plantations, condominiums, and shopping malls. It is they who relentlessly convert habitats needed by a multitude of species into habitat for one.

The relationship between people and other species with which we share the planet is a culturally prescribed one. The idea that our species might "manage" others is an acknowledgment of human dominance whose consequences reflect the view that prioritizes human needs and wants over the needs of all other species. This view so thoroughly permeates our culture that we find it expressed in theological interpretations, in such popular media as Hollywood movies, television, and pulp fiction, and in the loftier realms of literature, law, and science. It is a worldview that, coupled with capitalism, hierarchically arranges animal and plant species below humans, and assigns value based primarily on market price.

Yet there are those for whom alligators, fish, lakes, and marshes mean more than money. Their views are important because freshwater ecosystems contain tremendous biological diversity: Many species make a living in wetland, river, and lake environments. They matter because these ecosystems play a vital role in maintaining wider ecological health on which all species depend, including our own. And they matter because some of these fragile ecosystems, long treated as wastelands, are home to people whose worlds collectively constitute equally essential cultural diversity. People such as those in Shellcracker Haven offer knowledge and skills, social arrangements, and production systems that have allowed them to live in and from precious environments for generations. Together with the FWC and others who share an interest in the longevity of wild Florida, perhaps there is a way to save both rural communities and biodiversity, and so ourselves. After all, the bumper sticker is right: We all do live downstream.

Glossary

airboat a boat driven by a huge propeller caged and positioned at the back of the boat; used in waterways with heavy weed infestations, such as the Florida Everglades, and recreationally.

bag limit the number of game animals or fish that a licensed user is allowed to take by law; can be sex-, size-, and season-specific.

bang stick commercially or home-manufactured weapon; fires a shotgun shell from the end of a long stick or handle.

biodiversity biological diversity; the variety of life in all its forms, levels, and combinations; includes ecosystem diversity, species diversity, and genetic diversity.

bonnets local name given to water lilies whose leaves can sometimes fold in a way that makes them resemble a woman's bonnet.

bull gators male alligators; major contributors and supporters of the University of Florida football team.

carrying capacity the maximum number of individuals of a defined species that a given environment can support over the long term.

cast nets small nets thrown into shallow water to catch such things as small fish for bait.

CITES the Convention on International Trade in Endangered Species of Wild Fauna and Flora; an international agreement between governments, which are bound by its provisions, the aim of which is to ensure that international trade in specimens of wild animals and plants does not threaten their survival.

consumerism as used herein, the theory that a progressively greater consumption of goods is socially, psychologically, and economically beneficial.

crocodilian also *Crocodylian;* Linnaean taxonomic category for the order found within the class of carnivorous reptiles that includes the family alligatoridae (alligators and caimans) and the family crocodylidae (crocodiles).

eutrophication the process of oxygen depletion in a body of water caused by decaying organic matter.

exotic leathers tanned hides that feature prominently in the international fashion industry; they come from lizards, snakes, ostriches, elephants, and crocodilians; sold in many forms: tiny cosmetic cases, boots, briefcases, and golf bags, among others.

fish box a simple method for managing trotlines used in catfishing; the box is made of notched, square racks, stacked one on top of another into which trotlines, with hooks about every three feet, are fed before baiting. The box sits on a rotating spindle on the back of a boat so the line can be fed into the water one rack at a time.

fish house a building constructed near the dock and depot to accommodate the need for processing and icing down fish for shipment on the train.

game warden a person authorized to enforce hunting and fishing laws.

gig a pointed barb attached to a line and delivered from the end of a pole or spear into the skin of an alligator or frog.

jukes also called juke joints or honky-tonks; postemancipation establishments, often remote if not clandestine, where black laborers could congregate, dance, drink, gamble, and play the blues.

livelihood strategy the ways a person or family meets basic needs; can involve business ownership, management, or wage labor; barter; cash cropping; or subsistence production in horticulture, fishing, hunting, or scavenging—or, as is the usually the case, a combination of these.

monkey fishing an illegal technique for increasing the size of a catch by sending an electric current into the water, thereby stunning fish and causing them to float to the surface; became popular after seining became illegal in Florida.

naval stores industry   industry named for production of materials used in shipbuilding; products include rosin and turpentine, also known as mineral spirits.

Nuisance Alligator Control Program (NACP)   one of the program components of Florida's Alligator Management Program; established to remove alligators whose presence on highways, golf courses, swimming pools, private property, and other locations results in a complaint to the Florida Fish and Wildlife Conservation Commission.

panfish   edible fish species; includes bream, speckled perch, bluegills, shellcrackers, crappie, and others.

paper alligators   nonexistent farm alligators created illegally in bookkeeping to cover the practice of poaching wild alligators.

participant observers   a term that is used to describe social scientists working in the field to learn through firsthand experience and observation about a society.

rough fish   the name given to fish species that competes with desirable sports fish populations as well as marketable fish; not widely regarded as edible; includes gar, shad, and others.

sharecroppers   farmers who grow crops on others' land in exchange for a portion of the crops.

shiners   a popular baitfish harvested for sale and used by sports fishers in Florida.

still quarters   company-owned settlement built to house black families, one or more of whose members worked in the naval stores industry to produce turpentine from pine trees.

subsistence   what one needs to survive; subsistence production includes those activities in which whatever is produced is directly consumed by the producer's family rather than being sold or bartered.

trotlines   fishing lines, as long as 2,100 feet with hooks set about every 3 feet, used for commercial fishing in rivers and freshwater lakes; the technology permitted when the Florida Game and Fresh Water Fish Commission disallowed the use of seines.

urban sprawl   the physical pattern of low-density expansion of large urban areas under market conditions into surrounding rural areas; implies little planning, and is often patchy, scattered, and strung out, with a tendency to discontinuity because it leap-frogs over some areas, leaving agricultural enclaves; linked to social alienation and decline in the United States of a sense of community.

value-added conservation (VAC)   a theory that those with a vested interest in a natural resource, specifically an economic interest, will work to protect that resource.

wetland   transitional habitats between dry land and deep water; includes marshes, swamps, peat lands (including bogs and fens), flood meadows, lakes and ponds, rivers and streams, estuaries and other coastal waters including salt marshes, mangroves, and even coral reefs.

wetland mitigation   compensation for damage to or loss of a wetland in the form of restoration, creation of a replacement, or preservation of another wetland; *wetland mitigation banking* describes the Clinton era proposal to allow compensatory acts in anticipation of damage or destruction.

yeoman farm   a farm whose labor supply is made up of family members; produces largely for household consumption.

References

Allen, E. R., and W. T. Neill. 1949. Increasing Abundance of Alligators in the Eastern Portion of Its Range. *Herpetologia* 5(6):109–112.

Arensberg, Conrad, and Sol Kimball. 1965. *Culture and Community.* New York: Harcourt, Brace.

Ashby, John W. 1888. *Alachua: The Garden County of Florida: Its Resources and Advantages.* Alachua County Immigration Association. New York: South Publishing.

Bates, Daniel. 1996. *Cultural Anthropology.* Boston: Allyn and Bacon.

Dequine, John. 1948. Management of Florida's Fresh-Water Fisheries. *Transactions American Fisheries Society* 78:38–41.

Dequine, John. 1952. *Florida's Controlled Seining Program with a Discussion of General Fish Management Principles.* Fish Management Bulletin No. 1. Tallahassee, FL: Florida Game and Fresh Water Fish Commission.

Ewert, Alan W. (editor). 1996. *Natural Resource Management: The Human Dimension.* Boulder: Westview Press.

Florida Department of Agriculture and Consumer Services. n.d. *Alligator: An American Classic.* Louisiana Fur and Alligator Advisory Council and Division of Marketing, Aquaculture Market Development Aid Program.

Florida Fish and Wildlife Conservation Commission (FWC). 2002a. *Estimated Producer Value of Alligator Harvests on Florida Farms during 1977–2001.* Alligator Management Section, Bureau of Wildlife Resources, Division of Wildlife, Florida Fish and Wildlife Commission. Table 2. Farm Alligator Harvest Data. http://www.wildflorida.org/gators/farming.htm.

Florida Fish and Wildlife Conservation Commission (FWC). 2002b. *Private Lands Alligator Management Program Application Information Package.* Alligator Management Section, Bureau of Wildlife Resources, Division of Wildlife, Florida Fish and Wildlife Commission.

Florida Fish and Wildlife Conservation Commission (FWC). 2003a. *The Economic Value of Florida's Freshwater Fisheries.* Compiled by Bob Wattendorf. http://floridafisheries.com/updates/economic.html.

Florida Fish and Wildlife Conservation Commission (FWC). 2003b. *Law Enforcement: About FWC Law Enforcement.* http://floridaconservation.org/law/aboutus.htm.

Florida Game and Fresh Water Fish Commission (GFC). 1949. *Biennial Report. Biennium Ending December 31, 1948.* Tallahassee, FL: Florida Game and Fresh Water Fish Commission.

Florida Game and Fresh Water Fish Commission (GFC). 1968. *A Quarter Century of Progress: 1943–1968.* Tallahassee, FL: Florida Game and Fresh Water Fish Commission.

Florida Game and Fresh Water Fish Commission (GFC). 1980. *Annual Report, July 1, 1979–June 30, 1980.* Tallahassee, FL: Florida Game and Fresh Water Fish Commission.

Florida Game and Fresh Water Fish Commission (GFC). 1987. *Annual Report, 1984–1985.* Tallahassee, FL: Florida Game and Fresh Water Fish Commission.

Florida Game and Fresh Water Fish Commission (GFC). 1989. *Annual Report, 1987–1988.* Tallahassee, FL: Florida Game and Fresh Water Fish Commission.

Florida Game and Fresh Water Fish Commission (GFC). 1992. *Annual Report, 1990–1991.* Tallahassee, FL: Florida Game and Fresh Water Fish Commission.

Hardin, Garrett. 1968. The Tragedy of the Commons. *Science* 162:1243–1248.

Hill, Jesse O'Neal. 1950. *The Turpentine Industry: A Study Pertinent to*

Industrial Arts Instruction in the Secondary Schools. M.A. Thesis. Gainesville, FL: University of Florida.

Hines, T. C. 1979. The Past and Present Status of the Alligator in Florida. Proceedings of the Annual Conference. South East Association. *Fish and Wildlife Agencies* 33:224–232.

Jeffery, Roger, and Bhaskar Vira. 2001. Introduction. In *Conflict and Cooperation in Participatory Natural Resource Management,* Roger Jeffery and Bhaskar Vira, eds. New York: Palgrave. Pp. 1–17.

Kelly, W. D. 1888. *The Old South and the New.* New York: Putnam's.

Kersey, H. A. 1975. *Pelts, Plumes and Hides.* Gainesville, FL: University of Florida Press.

Kolankiewicz, Leon, and Roy Beck. 2001. *Sprawl in Florida.* www.sprawlcity.org/studyFL/index.html.

Lockie, Stewart, Vaughan Higgins, and Geoffrey Lawrence. 2001. What's Social About Natural Resources and Why Do We Need to Theorise It? In *Environment, Society, and Natural Resource Management,* Geoffrey Lawrence, Vaughan Higgins, and Stewart Lockie, eds. Northampton, MA: Edward Elgar. Pp. 1–15.

Luethy, Don R. 1956. *Survey Findings on the Lake George and St. Johns River Fisheries Investigations.* Tallahassee, FL: Florida Game and Fresh Water Fish Commission.

Murphy, M. n.d. Unpublished genealogy of the "Jameson" family.

Myers, O. A. 1882. *Alachua County: Her Attractive Features and Public Improvement.* Gainesville, FL: Cannon and McCreary.

Myers, Ronald L., and John J. Ewel. 1990. *Ecosystems of Florida.* Orlando: University of Central Florida Press.

Office of Program Policy Analysis and Government Accountability (OPPAGA). 2001. *Justification Review: Fish and Wildlife Conservation Commission.* Report No. 01–48.

Ostrum, Elinor. 1996. Crossing the Great Divide: Coproduction, Synergy, and Development. *World Development* 24:6.

Robinson, John G., and Kent H. Redford. 1991. The Use and Conservation of Wildlife. In *Neotropical Wildlife Use and Conservation,* John G. Robinson and Kent H. Redford, eds. Chicago: University of Chicago Press. Pp. 3–5.

Schroeder, Herbert W. 1996. Ecology of the Heart: Understanding How People Experience Natural Environments. In *Natural Resource Management: The Human Dimension,* Alan W. Ewert, ed. Boulder, CO: Westview Press.

Tebeau, Charlton W. 1971. *A History of Florida.* Coral Gables, FL: University of Miami Press.

U.S. Department of the Interior, Fish and Wildlife Service, and U.S. Department of Commerce, U.S. Census Bureau. 2002. *National Survey of Fishing, Hunting, and Wildlife-Associated Recreation. State Overview.* Washington, D.C. P. 17.

White, Lynn, Jr. 1967. The Historical Roots of Our Ecological Crisis. *Science* 155(3767):1203–1207.

Wondolleck, Julia. 1991. *Public Lands Conflict and Resolution: Managing National Forest Disputes.* New York: Plenum Press.

Woodward, Allen R., and Barry L. Cook. 2000. Nuisance-Alligator (*Alligator mississippiensis*) Control in Florida, U.S.A. In *Crocodiles. Proceedings of the 15th Working Meeting of the Crocodile Specialist Group.* Gland, Switzerland: IUCN-World Conservation Union. Pp. 446–455.

Woodward, Allen R., and Dennis N. David. 1994. Alligators. In *Prevention and Control of Wildlife Damage,* S. E. Hygnstrom, R. M. Timm, and G. E. Larson, eds. University of Nebraska. Pp. F1–F6.

Woodward, Allen R., and Michael F. Delany. 1987. American Alligator Management in Florida. In *Proceedings of the 3rd South Eastern Nongame and Endangered Wildlife Symposium,* R. R. Odom, K. A. Riddleberger, and S. C. Ozier, eds. Athens, GA.

Index